The Mixology of Astrology

COSMIC COCKTAIL RECIPES *for* EVERY SIGN

ALIZA KELLY FARAGHER

Adams Media

New York London Toronto Sydney New Delhi

To Emily Meade, for five thousand years of friendship; Annabel Gat,
for her cosmic guidance; Luke Schwartz, for his
profound patience; and my mother, Lotti Golden, for her teachings
in empathy, kindness, and magic. I love you.

Adams Media
An Imprint of Simon & Schuster, Inc.
57 Littlefield Street
Avon, Massachusetts 02322

Copyright © 2018 by Simon & Schuster, Inc.

All rights reserved, including the right to reproduce this book or portions thereof in any form whatsoever. For information address Adams Media Subsidiary Rights Department, 1230 Avenue of the Americas, New York, NY 10020.

First Adams Media hardcover edition August 2018

ADAMS MEDIA and colophon are trademarks of Simon & Schuster.

For information about special discounts for bulk purchases, please contact Simon & Schuster Special Sales at 1-866-506-1949 or business@simonandschuster.com.

The Simon & Schuster Speakers Bureau can bring authors to your live event. For more information or to book an event contact the Simon & Schuster Speakers Bureau at 1-866-248-3049 or visit our website at www.simonspeakers.com.

Interior design by Katrina Machado
Interior images © 123RF/angkrit chamchuen, monbibi, painterr; Getty Images/Berezka_Klo, painterr

Manufactured in the United States of America

10 9 8 7 6 5 4 3 2 1

Library of Congress Cataloging-in-Publication Data
Faragher, Aliza Kelly, author.
The mixology of astrology / Aliza Kelly Faragher.
Avon, Massachusetts: Adams Media, 2018.
Includes index.
LCCN 2018011479 (print) | LCCN 2018013256 (ebook) | ISBN 9781507208151 (hc) | ISBN 9781507208168 (ebook)
LCSH: Cocktails. | LCGFT: Cookbooks.
LCC TX951 (ebook) | LCC TX951 .F27 2018 (print) | DDC 641.87/4--dc23
LC record available at https://lccn.loc.gov/2018011479

ISBN 978-1-5072-0815-1
ISBN 978-1-5072-0816-8 (ebook)

Contents

3

Introduction

Are you an ambitious Capricorn facing down Mercury in retrograde? A temperamental Aries looking to soothe a short fuse? An optimistic Gemini celebrating a fresh start with the New Moon? There's a drink for that—and it's determined by your astrological sign.

You've probably checked out your horoscope to learn more about your love life, career prospects, and financial outlook. Well, the same convention works for cocktails too. Each astrological sign has unique drink favorites based on its personality traits, ranging from the aesthetic appeal to the flavors, and even the origins of the drink itself. By tapping into the tastes and traits of your zodiac sign, you can reveal the perfect cocktail for you.

The Mixology of Astrology is divided into thirteen sections and more than 175 carefully chosen recipes. In the first section, you'll learn about the basics of astrology and mixology, beginning with the history of the zodiac. You'll then explore the ins and outs of mixing a drink, from what bartending essentials you should always have on hand, to the best drinkware for every cocktail.

Each of the remaining twelve sections is devoted entirely to one astrological sign, where you'll find everything from the sign's personality quirks, to a variety of cocktail recipes that align with the distinct preferences of that sign. Are you a nonconformist Aquarius, searching for a signature drink that no one else will be sipping? Try a Cousin Vitamine. Are you a stylish Libra, in need of an eye-catching cocktail to pair with your ensemble? Look no further than the vibrant Appletini. And when your friends wonder how you always know their perfect drink, you can just tell them it was written in the stars...

So go ahead and pop the bubbly: may you discover new and existing dimensions of your sign through the adventure, creativity, and imagination of a fabulous cocktail!

The Cosmos, Straight Up: Blending Astrology and Mixology

Not an astrology guru? No idea what a "muddler" is? No worries! In this section, you will learn everything you need to know for understanding your sign and shaking a flawless martini. First, you will dive into the fascinating history of astrology and the twelve zodiac signs. Then, you will discover the different layers of your sign, from elements to quadruplicities (don't let the word scare you—it's less complicated than it seems!).

After you've got the astrology down, you'll explore the world of mixing drinks. From handy tools and drinkware to what exactly a "twist" is, you'll learn all of the basics for creating a perfect cocktail right at home. Ready, set, mix!

Stargazing: The Art of Looking Up

People have contemplated the stars for thousands of years. The Babylonians tracked the positions of celestial bodies such as the sun, and eventually divided the sky into twelve equal sections—the zodiac—with each area named after the main constellation that it contained. Ancient cultures later observed that when a planet passed through a section, there was a correlation between events on earth: babies born during that placement shared similar characteristics, and certain events were more likely to occur. These ideas were then adopted around 4 B.C.E. by the Greeks, who incorporated their mythology into the zodiac, laying the foundation for the horoscopic astrology used today. Though there are many working parts to modern astrology, the key to unlocking the unique traits of your sign is the sun.

Sun Signs

The most important thing when it comes to understanding your sign is the placement of the sun at your birth—specifically, which of the twelve constellations the sun was in when you were born. The placement of this vivid star reveals your sun sign, which symbolizes vitality and pride. (FYI: the sun sign is what all of those magazine quizzes and online horoscopes focus on.)

The sun sign reflects general personality traits, preferences, and "blind spots" in your character. If your sun sign is Taurus, you are steadfast and loyal, and tend to enjoy tactile activities that are rooted in reality (Taureans are great chefs, hairstylists, bankers, or project managers). But as a byproduct of your reliability, you can become quite stubborn, resisting change at all costs. As a Taurus, you love tantalizing the senses, so when it comes to cocktails, you will absolutely adore beverages like the decadent Icy Vanilla Rum Malted Milkshake and refreshingly tangy Pomegranate Martini.

Alternatively, if your sun sign is Pisces, you are sensitive and empathic, and thrive in creative, abstract pursuits (Pisceans are great musicians, designers, bartenders, or spiritual guides). Constantly absorbing energies and emotions, however, you can become easily overwhelmed, avoiding your responsibilities by swimming away. As a Pisces, you will love enchanting cocktails that perfectly capture your ethereal, dreamy spirit—from the refreshing Sea Breeze to the playful Surfer on Acid.

The sun also reveals the "hero's journey": the thematic backdrop of joys, pains, hopes, and hardships in a person's life. If your sun sign is Virgo, for instance, your themes involve intellectualism, kindness, perfectionism, and control. And as a Virgo, your distinctive ethos is reflected in your cocktail preferences! You will love straightforward beverages defined by their exquisite craftsmanship and fresh ingredients.

The sun signs are also divided into "triplicities" and "quadruplicities." These aspects of your sign can determine how you express your emotions and approach new situations.

The Elements: Fire, Earth, Air, and Water

"Triplicities" are the four elements of nature: fire, earth, air, and water. Fire signs (Aries, Leo, and Sagittarius) are passionate and vivacious, earth signs (Taurus, Virgo, and Capricorn) are reliable and logical, air signs (Gemini, Libra, and Aquarius) are intellectual and curious, and water signs (Cancer, Scorpio, and Pisces) are emotional and intuitive. If your element is earth, you will enjoy traditional cocktails like the Screwdriver and the Old-Fashioned (Capricorn). Alternatively, if your element is water, you will prefer potent and complex concoctions like the Mind Eraser (Pisces) and the Black Widow (Scorpio).

The Qualities: Cardinal, Fixed, and Mutable

Quadruplicities reflect the signs' qualities. Cardinal signs (Aries, Cancer, Libra, and Capricorn) kick off new seasons. These signs are excellent at taking action and starting new initiatives, but may be selfish in their pursuits. If your sign is cardinal, you will love sipping on the assertive Hot 'n' Sassy (Aries) and daring Jaded Lady (Capricorn). Fixed signs (Taurus, Leo, Scorpio, and Aquarius) occur in the middle of a season. These signs are consistent, steady forces that maintain movement, but have a tendency to be stubborn or rigid in their convictions. If your sign is fixed, you'll enjoy a sturdy Bloody Mary (Scorpio) and a tried-and-true Hot Toddy (Taurus). Lastly, mutable signs (Gemini, Virgo, Sagittarius, and Pisces) conclude seasons. These signs welcome growth through their adaptable spirits, but can also fear commitment and lack reliability. If your sign is mutable, try the playful Fuzzy Navel (Gemini) or find inner peace with the Zen Tea Cocktail (Pisces).

Ready to test your cosmic knowledge? Invite friends over for drinks at your place! You'll love matching delicious cocktails with your friends' unique astrological preferences. This astro bash will be a smash (I hope I'm invited!)—but before you start sending those texts, you'll need to learn a few bar basics.

Bar Grazing: The Art of Mixing It Up

Whatever your sign, we can all agree that cocktails are delicious. And while it's always fun to order drinks at a bar or restaurant, there's nothing like mixing up your own medicine. Just as it takes practice to become a skilled astrologer, there's also a learning curve when becoming a masterful at-home bartender. But you've got this—setting up shop is super easy!

The Tools

First, it's important to make sure you have all the necessary hardware for concocting the best beverages. So before you start showing off your fancy skills (I'm looking at you, Aries), invest in the following home-bar essentials:

- **Cocktail shaker:** The backbone of every James Bond martini, this classic device is used to quickly mix ingredients, including the ice that chills the beverage.
- **Mixing glass:** You'll use this clear pint glass for muddling ingredients and preparing liquids.
- **Jigger:** A jigger is a double-ended measuring tool that measures both 1 ounce and 1½ ounces of liquid.
- **Citrus juicer:** This tool will help you get the most bang for your grocery buck.
- **Strainer:** You can use either a Hawthorne strainer (if you're using a Boston Shaker) or a fine-mesh strainer.
- **Muddler:** This stick made of wood or plastic is used for extracting those delicious essential oils from ingredients (pro tip: you can also use the back of a wooden spoon).
- **Bar spoon:** Designed to reach the bottom of tall glasses, this long-handled spoon ensures a professional swirl every time.
- **Ice cube tray:** Avoid an embarrassing face-palm moment by making sure you're stocked with ice *before* preparing your favorite beverage.

The Drinkware

After you're set up with the hardware, the next step is glassware. There are a *lot* of vessels out there, but if you're just starting out, the following glasses are used for the most classic drinks, as well as the recipes you'll find throughout this book:

- **Old-Fashioned (or "Rocks") Glass:** Holds 6–8 ounces; designed for "building" drinks (adding each ingredient and stirring the contents in the glass—as opposed to pouring in the contents after using a cocktail shaker or mixing glass). Traditionalist Capricorns will especially want to have this glass handy!
- **Cocktail (or "Martini") Glass:** Holds 3–5 ounces; designed to serve "up" cocktails (drinks shaken in a shaker and strained into a glass without ice).
- **Highball (or "Collins") Glass:** Holds 8–16 ounces; designed to serve "tall" drinks that contain a large proportion of nonalcoholic mixers poured over ice.
- **Margarita Glass:** Holds 10–16 ounces; designed to serve its namesake cocktail or other fruity drinks. Are you fun-loving Leos paying attention?
- **Hurricane Glass:** Holds 15–20 ounces; designed to serve tropical drinks.
- **Irish Coffee Glass (or "Irish Coffee Mug"):** Holds 6–12 ounces; designed to serve hot beverages.
- **Shot Glass:** Holds 1 ounce; designed to serve "shooters" (drinks swallowed in one gulp).
- **Champagne Flute:** Holds 6 ounces; designed to serve carbonated beverages.
- **Coupe Flute:** Holds 4–6 ounces, designed to serve aesthetic cocktails.
- **Red Wine Glass:** Holds 8–12 ounces; designed with a balloon-shaped bowl to release the aromas of red wine. Taureans will be especially glad they have this glass, which is perfect for sampling through all five senses!

- **White Wine Glass:** Holds 8–12 ounces; designed with a slim bowl to preserve the temperature of chilled white wine.
- **Pint Glass:** Holds 16 ounces; designed to serve beer.

Now that your cabinet is stocked with sparkling glassware, you're almost ready to show off your collection. But will you be ready if one of your guests pops the question? No, not that one. An even more important query…

Shaken or Stirred?

Though some drinks are built directly into the glass, most cocktails are either shaken or stirred, so it's critical to understand the difference between these two processes.

Generally speaking, cocktails to shake include fruit juices, cream liqueurs, simple syrup, sour mixes, eggs, dairy, or any other creamy modifier (an ingredient that is not the primary liquor). Shaking creates a cloudy appearance and breaks down the ice of the beverage, resulting in a blended, textured sip. Cocktails to stir, however, include distilled spirits or light mixers. Stirring is a gentler technique that preserves the ice, adding significantly less water to the drink, and thus maintaining the drink's potency.

Speaking of strength, it's important to know how much punch your drinks are packing—yes, this includes you, Scorpio! Though amateur mixers (namely college students) "eyeball" a drink "to taste," this naïve logic is faulty. Too much or too little of an ingredient can radically change a recipe, ruining a delicious cocktail. Alternatively, if a liquid experiment turns out to be absolutely incredible, it will be impossible to replicate the libation without knowing the proportions! Fortunately, bar measurements are easy to follow.

Mixing Up the Medicine: Bar Measurements

The truth is, the components of a cocktail are only as good as a bartender's preparation. A drink can boast the finest spirits in the world, but if the ingredients are thrown together haphazardly, the cocktail will taste...well, disgusting. Though fancy cocktail-shaking techniques require practice (and, surprisingly, muscle!), heeding proportions is straightforward—no extravagant wrist tricks required. Below is a handy table detailing key bar measurements for perfect cocktails.

BARTENDER MEASURES		
Bar Measurements	Standard	Metric
1 pinch	0.03 ounce	0.44 milliliter
1 dash	0.25 ounce	0.9 milliliter
1 splash	0.5 ounce	7.5 milliliters
1 float	0.015 ounce	14.8 milliliters

Many of these bar measurements punctuate cocktails by capturing a unique look and feel: a beverage can be radically transformed by a pinch, dash, float, or splash.

The Garnish: Lemons, Cherries, and Olives—Oh My!

Garnishes are also used to enhance beverages. Though their significance may be surprising, ornamental accents actually have a time-honored place in cocktail history. That's right, darling Libras, your favorite decadent garnishes are an essential component of mixology!

Even the earliest bartenders' manuals (dating back to the 1860s) describe the unique accents of different cocktails. While utilitarian-minded drinkers (*ahem*—Virgo) may dismiss them as purely indulgent, garnishes actually serve practical purposes. Not only do garnishes define a drink's physical appearance—separating a given concoction from any others that share its primary ingredients—they also inform a beverage's flavor profile by adding hints of taste and fragrance. Though the influence appears subtle, zesty, fruity, and flowery embellishments infuse the beverage and enhance the entire sipping experience.

Though you are certainly free to experiment with trimmings of your own (freethinking Sagittarians won't need to hear that twice!), many recipes (especially classic ones) specify precise garnishes. Here are the traditional bartending terms for these elegant adornments:

- **Twist:** A twisted strip of a citrus fruit's outer peel ("zest").
- **Slice (also "Wheel"):** A flat, round slice of citrus.
- **Peel:** A piece of citrus zest.
- **Flamed peel:** A piece of citrus zest lit on fire to enhance its aromatic properties.
- **Cube:** A square piece of fruit.
- **Wedge:** A citrus wedge.

Armed with the astrology and bar essentials, you're ready to explore how these two ideas are linked. Now that deserves a toast!

As Above, So Below: The Universe, with a Twist

Now that you have the basics of both astrology *and* mixology down (an impressive combination, I might add), you're ready to start combining your practices! Astrology and mixology are a perfectly suited pair: just as each sun sign reveals personal tastes and traits, cocktails offer unique flavor profiles that appeal to different preferences. Let's look at a couple of examples...

Aquarians are freethinkers who aspire to change the world, making revolutionary cocktails like the Cuba Libre or provocative drinks such as Agent Orange the perfect choice for these rebellious signs. Gemini, on the other hand, are the social butterflies of the zodiac. Gemini love cocktails with wild names that tell fantastic stories, making the compelling Harvey Wallbanger and bizarre Monkey Gland the ideal concoctions for this buoyant air sign.

So whether you're throwing a party or simply mixing up a refreshing beverage for a friend, all you need to reveal the perfect cocktail for each sign is a date of birth. Well, what are you waiting for: what's your sign?

Aries

(MARCH 21–APRIL 19): THE WARRIOR

Aries is the first sign of the zodiac. Its astrological placement comes as no surprise—fearless rams are *always* number one. Aries spark the match that ignites action, and are known for their energetic, youthful spontaneity and high-intensity approach to life.

Celestial rams are ruled by Mars, the planet that governs ambition and determination, so this energetic fire sign thrives on challenges, competition, and invigorating opportunities. Aries don't do demure; these confident and courageous rams are natural leaders, so passionate Aries aren't afraid to take charge and get things done. Aries attract friends and lovers with their natural enthusiasm and optimism, spicing up all relationships through their contagious joie de vivre.

When it comes to cocktails, Aries love taking risks. Don't even bother trying to tantalize Aries with dull beverages: an uninspiring glass of vino or a humdrum vodka soda is a total snoozefest for these passionate fire signs. When ordering or preparing a cocktail, consider bold colors, rich flavors, and shameless reputations. These fire signs enjoy beverages that match their adventurous and spirited personalities. Are you brave enough to order a jalapeño-infused Spicy Margarita, or an infamous Alabama Slammer? Thrill-seeking Aries will gladly accept this dare!

Alabama Slammer

Rambunctious rams are naturally attracted to cocktails with equally rowdy reputations, so they will absolutely adore the Alabama Slammer. This southern specialty is rumored to have been invented at the University of Alabama in 1975, making the beverage an ideal complement to Lynyrd Skynyrd's iconic anthem, "Sweet Home Alabama." This Deep South drink grew popular quickly, becoming a hit with college crowds during the 1980s. A well-prepared Alabama Slammer boasts a stunning crimson hue reminiscent of the university's primary school color. It's hard for adventurous Aries to resist the draw of this down-home drink. Even if the University of Alabama is not your alma mater, Aries, you will be sure to love this collegiate classic.

SERVES 1

1 ounce Southern Comfort
1 ounce sloe gin
1 ounce amaretto

Orange juice to fill
Orange slice, seeded, for garnish
Maraschino cherry, for garnish

Combine all ingredients except garnishes in a shaker filled with ice. Shake, and strain into a highball glass filled with fresh ice. Class up this dormitory drink by garnishing with orange slice and cherry, and get ready for some heavy-duty southern revelry!

Apple Fizz

Aries despise boredom. These restless rams are always seeking new adventures and unique ways to spice up their routines. The Apple Fizz is a terrific way to give new life to the classic champagne cocktail. By simply adding apple juice to their favorite glass of champagne, Aries can create a dynamic, flavorful cocktail.

SERVES 1

1 (25-ounce) bottle champagne
1 ounce apple juice
Apple slice, for garnish

Fill a champagne flute three-quarters of the way with champagne. Add apple juice. Garnish with apple slice, and get ready to clink glasses!

Bishop Cocktail

Not much of a wine connoisseur? Don't fret, dear Aries! Even your classiest acquaintances will be impressed by the Bishop Cocktail. Once you master the recipe, you'll enjoy sharing this sensual blend of red wine, rum, and simple syrup. Originally invented in New York in the 1930s, this urbane cocktail is a perfect way to toast any celebration. Cheers!

SERVES 1

3 ounces dark rum
1 ounce dry red wine
1 teaspoon simple syrup
½ ounce lime juice

Chill a red wine glass in the freezer for five minutes. Pour ingredients into a cocktail shaker filled with ice. Shake well and pour into chilled glass. Who knew sipping vino could be *this* much fun!

Blue Hawaii

Aries love to stand out in a crowd, making the neon-colored Blue Hawaii a perfectly suited cocktail for this bold fire sign. Invented by bartender Harry Yee, who popularized the tiki bar craze of the 1950s and 1960s, this distinctively azure beverage has been a vacation staple for over half a century. Rumor has it that Yee experimented with several versions before settling on this cerulean delight. Playful Aries will enjoy sipping this beachside libation and, in fact, may find themselves twisting like Elvis Presley (he was, after all, the star of the eponymous 1961 film)...lei and ukulele optional.

SERVES 1

3 ounces pineapple juice
1 ounce light rum
1 ounce vodka
1 ounce blue curaçao

½ ounce sweet-and-sour mix
Pineapple cube, for garnish
Maraschino cherry, for garnish
Cocktail umbrella, for garnish

Combine all ingredients except garnishes in a shaker filled with ice. Vigorously shake. Strain into a hurricane glass over ice, and garnish with pineapple cube, maraschino cherry, and cocktail umbrella to create the perfect island ambiance. At last—paradise found!

Boozy Hot Chocolate

Even in the cold weather months, Aries are always looking to heat things up. Boozy Hot Chocolates are the perfect after-dinner treat for a wintry night, and a fun way for Aries to explore their wild side during a traditionally quiet evening. Youthful Aries love feeling like a kid (in fact, many Aries look much younger than their age), and this combination of their favorite childhood ingredients (chocolate and mini marshmallows)—with a kick—will be sure to arouse their inner child!

SERVES 1

2 ounces finely chopped semisweet chocolate
6 ounces hot milk

1½ ounces Irish cream liqueur
4 mini marshmallows, for garnish

Place chopped semisweet chocolate in an Irish coffee glass. Pour hot milk over chocolate, and let stand for two minutes before stirring with a spoon until smooth. Add Irish cream liqueur, and stir to combine flavors. Garnish with mini marshmallows for a charming presentation—no mittens required!

Brandy Sour

The Brandy Sour has an esteemed place in cocktail history. This classic, refreshing beverage dates back to the 1930s, and is defined by its sneaky history. This cocktail originated in Cyprus, when visiting King Farouk of Egypt requested a boozy—yet discreet—alternative to the iced tea served at his hotel. To accommodate the regal guest, the hotel's bartenders invented the Brandy Sour. This tart concoction proved to be the perfect solution: its understated golden hue is complemented by distinctive citrus flavors that effortlessly capture the essence of the Mediterranean. The Brandy Sour quickly became a regional favorite. In fact, the drink is so iconic that it is now considered the unofficial cocktail of Cyprus. Aries will appreciate the Brandy Sour's elusive origins, and will love its delicious taste (perfect for any time of day!).

SERVES 1

2 ounces brandy
¾ ounce fresh lemon juice
¾ ounce simple syrup

Lemon slice, seeded, for garnish
Maraschino cherry, for garnish

Chill a martini glass in the freezer for five minutes. Combine all ingredients except garnishes in a shaker filled with ice. Shake vigorously and strain into chilled cocktail glass. Class it up with a lemon slice and maraschino cherry garnish. Very sophisticated, Aries darling!

Hot 'n' Sassy

Aries are enchanted by anything shiny and new, so the Hot 'n' Sassy is an ideal cocktail for these cutting-edge rams. A fairly recent creation, this cheeky beverage may not be familiar to many mixologists and bartenders. The cocktail's name alone captures Aries' spirit, which is widely recognized for its fiery sensibilities. This contemporary concoction combines vodka, jalapeños, and citrus with lemon-lime soda for an exhilarating experience guaranteed to raise the pulse. Aries will love impressing their friends with this fresh cocktail, perhaps even proclaiming it as the ram's unofficial signature drink.

SERVES 1

3 jalapeño slices, seeded
2 clementine slices, seeded
1 ounce vodka

1 ounce lemon-lime soda
½ ounce lime juice

Use muddler or the base of a wooden spoon to muddle jalapeño and clementine slices in a cocktail shaker. Add vodka and ice and shake vigorously. Pour into a highball glass filled with fresh ice, lemon-lime soda, and lime juice. Stir, sip, and enjoy!

Kamikaze

The Kamikaze is one of the most famed—and feared—cocktails in modern mixology. This libation was widely popular during the 1970s disco era, when nightclub-goers would sip this powerful concoction for a dose of liquid courage on the dance floor. Though the Kamikaze's notorious potency is not for the faint of heart, this cocktail is no big deal for fearless Aries. In fact, these bold rams are already bursting with exuberant energy, making the Kamikaze cocktail the ideal match for Aries' vibrant spirit. Turn up the music when you serve this dangerously delicious creation, dearest Aries, and you'll be sure to boogie all night long.

SERVES 1

1½ ounces vodka
¾ ounce triple sec

¾ ounce lime juice

Chill a martini glass in the freezer for five minutes. Combine all ingredients in a shaker filled with ice. Shake (*your groove thang*), and strain into chilled martini glass.

Long Island Iced Tea

Ahh, yes, the notorious Long Island Iced Tea. This heavy-duty cocktail combines five kinds of liquor, so its reputation is well deserved. While other signs may balk at the mere thought of this beverage, Aries willingly embraces it. In fact, just like Aries, the Long Island Iced Tea is loud, bold, and sure to cause a scene! Though this drink is associated with the main goal of instant, um, tipsiness, the Long Island Iced Tea can be quite the tasty pick-me-up. But proceed with caution, darling ram, and don't say we didn't warn you!

SERVES 1

½ ounce triple sec
½ ounce light rum
½ ounce gin
½ ounce gold tequila

1 ounce sour mix
7 ounces cola
Lemon wedge, for garnish

Pour the spirits and sour mix into a Collins glass filled with ice. Stir well and add cola. Garnish with a lemon wedge to complete the iced tea image. Sip (slowly!) and enjoy!

Michelada

Aries enjoy leading the way, sharing their favorite unique brewskies while kicking back with friends. Micheladas are a clever, easy way to spice up your favorite Mexican beer. As natural go-getters, Aries will love jazzing up cervezas (beer) with their own blend of ingredients, adding heat to a refreshing cold brew. This summertime favorite is easy to make, and even easier to drink. A perfect daytime beverage, Micheladas are rumored to cure even the toughest hangovers. So if you're desperately seeking the "hair of the dog," look no further than this creative lager.

SERVES 1

2 lime wedges, divided
Kosher salt
Cayenne pepper
½ ounce lime juice
2 drops Tabasco sauce

2 dashes Worcestershire sauce
Pinch ground black pepper
Pinch celery salt
1 (12-ounce) can Mexican lager
  beer

Rub a lime wedge along half the rim of a pint glass, then dip the top of the glass into a mixture of equal parts salt and cayenne pepper. Combine the remaining ingredients in the glass, adding the beer last. Garnish with the remaining lime wedge for a citrusy flair.

Orgasm

Motivated by their desires, Aries are known for being quite passionate. The Orgasm can be too hot to handle, but it should be no surprise that it serves as the ultimate elixir for sensual rams. A tantalizing combination of four liquors in equal parts, the Orgasm is designed to deliver a smooth, creamy taste. Why the name? This beverage is so easy to drink that its intoxicating power creeps up slowly, resulting in a totally unexpected euphoric experience. Double the recipe for twice the fun! Adventurous Aries will keep the party going well into the night, sharing this enticing concoction with friends and lovers alike.

SERVES 1

½ ounce white crème de cacao
½ ounce amaretto
½ ounce triple sec

½ ounce vodka
½ ounce whole milk

Chill a martini glass in the freezer for five minutes. Combine all ingredients in a shaker filled with ice. Shake vigorously and strain into chilled martini glass. How seductive!

Rum Swizzle

Adventurous Aries love a good time, and what is more fun than a delicious summertime libation for you and your friends? Though it may sound like a fancy (and extremely challenging) dance move, the Rum Swizzle is an easy-to-make refreshment rooted in the tropics. Guaranteed to appeal to the swashbuckling pirate within, this beverage gets its snazzy name from its preparation technique: the original swizzle sticks featured long stems with multiple prongs jutting out horizontally, and were snapped off of trees in the Caribbean! When twirled rapidly inside a cold cocktail, the swizzle stick creates a thick frost on the outside of the glass.

SERVES 4

8 ounces pineapple juice
8 ounces orange juice
8 ounces dark rum
¾ ounce grenadine

6 dashes bitters
4 orange slices, seeded, for garnish
4 pineapple cubes, for garnish
4 maraschino cherries, for garnish

Combine all ingredients except garnishes in a pitcher filled one-third of the way with crushed ice. With an authentic (or modern plastic) swizzle stick, stir the concoction vigorously until it froths (as an alternative, you can also shake in a large shaker). When ready, strain into four rocks glasses filled with fresh ice. Keep the vibes extra beachy by adding an orange slice, pineapple cube, and maraschino cherry garnish to each glass. Delicious!

Spicy Margarita

Is there any beverage more quintessentially Aries than a Spicy Margarita? Even without the added heat, Margaritas mirror the archetypal Aries spirit: they're iconic, playful, and known to induce untamable rowdiness. With added spice, however, Margaritas get an extra dose of fabulous. The Spicy Margarita cocktail is tart and exquisitely zesty—a perfect companion for warm-weather revelry. In fact, spicy refreshments are actually proven to provide a cooling effect on hot days. That's right, darling Aries, you now have a terrific excuse to enjoy this refreshing beverage all summer long!

SERVES 1

2 jalapeño slices, seeded
½ ounce agave syrup
1½ ounces silver tequila

1 ounce lime juice
½ ounce triple sec

Use muddler or the base of a wooden spoon to muddle seedless jalapeño slices and agave syrup in a cocktail shaker. Pour in the remaining ingredients and fill with ice. Shake until chilled, and strain into a rocks glass filled with fresh ice. Now that's *delicioso*!

Strawberry Mint Spritzer

Aries attract lots of friends with their dynamic exuberance and thrilling impulsivity. In fact, these fire signs are natural leaders who enjoy building communities and surrounding themselves with fun, inspiring, and ambitious people. When hosting a party, Aries will love serving Strawberry Mint Spritzers. These easy beverages are the ideal cocktail for any event, combining the fresh flavors of strawberry, mint, and lemon with smooth sake and bubbly champagne. Aries will enjoy both preparing and sipping these tangy and fresh treats, and this delicious concoction is perfect for a summertime barbecue, outdoor party, or spontaneous hang.

SERVES 6

1 pint strawberries, hulled, sliced, and divided

4 fresh mint leaves

6 small lemons, wedged

1 (25-ounce) bottle sake

1 (25-ounce) bottle champagne

Put six strawberry slices to the side for garnish. Add remaining strawberry slices and mint leaves to a large pitcher (make sure your pitcher is not made of thin glass, as it can crack during the next step). Squeeze juice from lemons and carefully muddle the ingredients with a muddler or the base of a wooden spoon. Fill the pitcher with ice and add equal parts sake and champagne. Stir vigorously, making sure the flavors are equally distributed. Pour into six rocks glasses and garnish each with a fresh strawberry slice. Now break out the lawn chairs and wide-brimmed hats: it's time for some unadulterated warm-weather fun!

Whiskey Smash

Warrior Aries are known for their courage, but watch out for their explosive tempers! When angered, these intrepid rams suddenly transform into the Hulk, destroying absolutely everything in sight. Fortunately, Aries' outbursts don't last long, and the Whiskey Smash is the perfect cocktail to help short-fused Aries get back in touch with their playful side. Aries will appreciate cooling off with the refreshing citrus flavors of a Whiskey Smash, guiding these fire signs from savage to soothed, and quickly restoring their exuberant, fun-loving dispositions.

SERVES 1

½ small lemon, wedged
2 ounces bourbon whiskey

¾ ounce simple syrup
4 fresh mint leaves, divided

In a shaker, muddle lemon using a muddler or the base of a wooden spoon. Add remaining ingredients (except one mint leaf for garnish) and fill shaker with ice. Shake and double-strain into a rocks glass filled with crushed ice. Garnish with mint leaf and serve with a straw. Ahh...that tantrum was *definitely* worth it!

White Russian

Aries love anything novel, so these fiery rams will adore the White Russian's potent punch and creamy texture, rich with retro revival. The White Russian is a classic three-ingredient cocktail that is flavorful, decadent, and boasts a major cult following. Introduced in the 1960s, when cream was added to the historic Black Russian, it had a few years of popularity, though it eventually faded into obscurity after becoming associated with uncool "squares." This all changed in 1998 when the blockbuster hit *The Big Lebowski* sparked a cult following: the film's protagonist continually slurped White Russians, creating a newfound interest in this velvety libation.

SERVES 1

2 ounces vodka
1 ounce coffee liqueur
1 ounce heavy cream

Pour vodka and coffee liqueur into a rocks glass filled with ice. Slowly fill the glass with heavy cream and stir. The Dude abides.

Taurus

(APRIL 20–MAY 20): THE LUXURIANT

Have you ever spent several hours soaking in a tub filled with essential oils and flower petals, surrounded by fragrant candles and the soothing sounds of classical music? Those born under the Taurus constellation certainly have! These celestial bulls are ruled by Venus (the planet that governs love, beauty, and money), making Taurus the most sensual sign of the zodiac. Taureans enjoy tantalizing the senses through soft fabrics, rich cuisines, and intoxicating aromas. But don't be fooled: these pleasure-seeking bulls also know the value of a dollar.

Taurus is an earth sign, so despite these bulls' hedonistic tendencies, Taureans are logical and financially responsible (though there's *always* a budget for facial cream). Taureans are steadfast friends and loyal lovers, and are committed to living their best lives.

These decadent bulls are known for their refined palates, and appreciate robust libations that capture a profusion of flavors, textures, and scents. Whether warming up with a toasty Hot Toddy or savoring the smoky essence of an eccentric Bacontini, Taureans enjoy cocktails that create a truly enveloping experience. Take note: when mixing up a beverage for your Taurus friend or lover, be sure to avoid cheap, poor-quality liquors. Though premium spirits may be a bit more costly, sensory Taureans can taste the difference. Their tastes can be expensive, but celestial bulls appreciate when their sophisticated palates are honored.

Bacontini

Taureans are the foodies of the zodiac, and these gourmands know the bacon craze is well founded: bacon's distinctive savory essence adds delicious complexity to a wide variety of dishes. Now Taurean bacon lovers can expand their horizons even further: behold, the Bacontini! Though a bit eccentric in both name and presentation, the Bacontini is an incredibly scrumptious libation that indulgent bulls will absolutely adore. The perfect Bacontini requires infused vodka that captures the meat's smoky, tangy quality. But don't fret: "bacon vodka" is readily available and, with such a captivating flavor, will make a great addition to your liquor cabinet.

SERVES 1

6 ounces bacon-infused vodka
1 tablespoon olive brine (from jar of olives)
2 teaspoons dry vermouth
3 pimiento-stuffed green olives, for garnish

Chill a martini glass in the freezer for five minutes. Combine infused vodka, brine, and vermouth in a shaker filled with ice. Shake vigorously and strain into chilled martini glass. Garnish with three olives threaded on a toothpick, and enjoy your totally fabulous Bacontini!

Between the Sheets

Sexy, sensual Taurus is one of the most romantic signs of the zodiac. These celestial bulls are ruled by Venus, the planet that governs romance and love. Erotic Taureans will love sipping on this provocatively named cocktail, which has a long history, dating back to the 1930s. It is believed that this cocktail was first invented in Paris as an aperitif. Rumors aside, it is certain that this scandalizing beverage's balanced mixture of rum, triple sec, and cognac has continued to enchant cocktail connoisseurs for generations.

SERVES 1

1 ounce cognac
1 ounce triple sec
1 ounce light rum

¼ ounce lemon juice
Flamed orange peel,
    for garnish

Chill a cocktail glass in the freezer for five minutes. Combine all ingredients except garnishes in a cocktail shaker filled with ice. Shake, and strain into chilled cocktail glass. For an extra-provocative kick, flame an orange peel over the glass and discard before serving. Is it hot in here, or is it just me?

Blenheim

Sensual Taureans love tastes, scents, and aromas, so it's no surprise that one of the most iconic mixologists, Joe Gilmore, was born under the Taurus constellation. During his time at the Savoy Hotel's American Bar in London, Gilmore invented numerous cocktails and prepared drinks for celebrities, politicians, and royalty. One of Gilmore's most popular cocktails, the Blenheim, was created for Sir Winston Churchill's ninetieth birthday. The combination of brandy, Chartreuse, and Lillet creates a distinctive, sophisticated flavor appreciated by gourmands and cocktail connoisseurs. Taureans will love the Blenheim's complex richness, while appreciating the historical significance of this timeless classic.

SERVES 1

1 ounce brandy
½ ounce Yellow Chartreuse
¼ ounce Lillet
¼ ounce Dubonnet
¼ ounce orange juice

Combine all ingredients in a cocktail shaker filled with ice and shake vigorously. Strain into a martini glass and enjoy!

Boulevardier

Taureans will love this historic beverage that exudes sophistication. Simple, yet extremely distinctive, the Boulevardier dates back to the 1920s. It is a close relative of the Negroni cocktail, but uses whiskey instead of gin. Though this beverage almost faded into obscurity during the mid-twentieth century, it has experienced an enormous comeback in recent years due to the accessibility of its ingredients, easy-to-follow preparation, and dynamic flavor profile. The warmth of the whiskey combined with the zest of the Campari creates a complex, rich flavor perfect for cool autumn nights.

SERVES 1

1¼ ounces whiskey

1 ounce Campari

1 ounce sweet vermouth

Orange twist, for garnish

Combine all ingredients except garnish in a rocks glass filled with fresh ice and stir to combine. Garnish with orange twist and voilà: a Boulevardier! *Très chic!*

Brave Bull

What could be more perfect for an earthy Taurus than the Brave Bull cocktail? Celestial bulls will adore the concept (Taureans are extremely courageous), as well as the concoction itself. The Brave Bull is a tequila-based version of a Black Russian, and is the ideal happy hour refreshment. Tequila's agave base creates a strong, complex flavor that enhances the java taste, delivering a well-balanced beverage. Taureans will love the boldness of this cocktail, and with such an apropos name, it may very well become the bull's signature drink!

SERVES 1

2 ounces silver tequila
1 ounce coffee liqueur

Pour silver tequila into a rocks glass filled with large ice cubes, and slowly add coffee liqueur. Swirl glass gently, or lightly stir, to mix ingredients.

Bull's Eye

Uh-oh! You've invited your friends over for cocktail night, but just realized you're out of booze! The nearest liquor store is closed, and all you have in the fridge are a few cans of light beer. What are you going to do?! Fear not, darling Taurus! The Bull's Eye is the perfect beer-based solution. The Bull's Eye effortlessly transforms your favorite light brewskies into dynamic, elegant libations that are perfect for every occasion. Ginger ale and sugar enhance the flavors of the beer, while lemon juice creates zesty, tangy notes that are guaranteed to tickle your taste buds. The Bull's Eye is so wonderful, in fact, that you may find yourself swapping your favorite liquor cocktails for this clever, fizzy concoction.

SERVES 2

⅓ cup lemon juice

1 (12-ounce) can light beer

1 (12-ounce) can ginger ale

2 tablespoons granulated sugar

Pour lemon juice into a pitcher, followed by beer and ginger ale. Add sugar and stir until it dissolves. Pour into two highball glasses filled with ice. Cheers, Taurus, you've saved the day! Now that's what I call hitting the bull's eye!

Champagne Cocktail

Though responsible Taureans know they can't *always* live like Marie Antoinette (after all, she was beheaded), the Champagne Cocktail is the perfect accessory when Taurus is feeling extra luxurious. This modern twist will bedazzle your favorite glass of bubbly by adding sugar and bitters. After a few sips, you may even feel inspired to proclaim, "Let them eat cake!"...or just have a few bites yourself.

SERVES 1

1 sugar cube
2 dashes bitters
4 ounces champagne
Lemon twist, for garnish

Place sugar cube on a spoon and douse with bitters. Drop cube into a flute glass, and add champagne. Garnish with a lemon twist and prepare to luxuriate!

Chocolate Coffee Cooler

What could possibly improve the combination of chocolate and coffee? Booze, of course! Taureans will love preparing (and drinking!) Chocolate Coffee Coolers. These decadent combinations of vodka, coffee liqueur, ice cream, and chocolate-covered espresso beans are the perfect late-night treat to truly satisfy the senses.

SERVES 1

1½ ounces coffee liqueur
1 ounce vodka
¼ cup chocolate-covered espresso beans, divided
½ cup chocolate ice cream

Combine all ingredients (except three espresso beans for garnish) in a blender and blend until smooth. Pour into a hurricane glass and garnish with remaining chocolate-covered espresso beans. Yum!

Daiquiri

Though Taureans love to relax, these celestial bulls also have a wild side. And when they are ready to turn up, they surely look to the classic Daiquiri cocktail. Throughout the 1940s, whiskey and vodka were difficult to obtain due to rationing during World War II. At the same time, Franklin D. Roosevelt's "Good Neighbor Policy" opened trade between the United States, Latin America, and the Caribbean, resulting in a rise of rum-based drinks. The Daiquiri quickly became a happy hour staple, and continues to deliver as a party favorite. This refreshing libation combines rum, lime juice, and simple syrup to create the perfect tangy treat. Taureans will love this time-honored favorite that has been spicing up parties for generations.

SERVES 1

2 ounces light rum
1 ounce lime juice
1 ounce simple syrup
Lime slice, seeded, for garnish

Chill a martini glass in the freezer for five minutes. Combine all ingredients except garnish in a shaker filled with ice. Shake, and strain into chilled martini glass. Garnish with a lime slice and get ready to have some fun!

Gold Rush

Within astrology, the Taurus constellation represents the material world, including luxury items and money. That's right, cosmic warriors, Taureans love surrounding themselves with grandeur, and these celestial bulls will be sure to strike it rich with the Gold Rush cocktail. Named after the historic period that brought some 300,000 settlers to California (now appropriately nicknamed "The Golden State"), this delectable refreshment combines bourbon, lemon juice, and honey to create a beautiful, golden-hued beverage. Its elegant presentation, combined with its smooth flavor profile, will be sure to cause any Taurus to cry out "Eureka!" on the very first sip.

SERVES 1

2 ounces bourbon
¾ ounce lemon juice
¾ ounce honey
Maraschino cherry, for garnish

Combine bourbon, lemon juice, and honey in a cocktail shaker filled with ice. To dissolve honey, shake vigorously for twenty seconds. Strain into a rocks glass with one large ice cube, and garnish with a maraschino cherry for a tasteful adornment.

Hot Toddy

The warm, aromatic, and effortlessly delicious Hot Toddy is the perfect beverage for fancy Taureans who love to shamelessly indulge their senses. The Hot Toddy is a classic hot cocktail that has been used to provide comfort and warmth in cold climates for centuries. In fact, this beverage is one of the oldest cocktails still being enjoyed today—its origins date back to the 1700s! It's no surprise that this classic beverage has withstood the test of time: just a few sips of this soothing elixir will create instant warmth from the inside out. Venusian Taureans will love snuggling up on the couch with a soft blanket and toasty Hot Toddy, slipping into the ultimate cozy evening.

SERVES 1

Hot water to fill an Irish coffee glass, divided

4 whole cloves

Lemon twist

2 teaspoons brown sugar

½ ounce lemon juice

2 ounces whiskey

Fill an Irish coffee glass with hot water. Let stand for a minute or two while sticking cloves into lemon twist. Set aside. Empty the glass and fill halfway with fresh hot water (this technique helps set the perfect temperature for both the glass and beverage). Add sugar and stir to dissolve. Add prepared lemon twist and continue stirring. Stir in lemon juice and whiskey. Now get ready for a warm whiskey embrace!

Icy Vanilla Rum Malted Milkshake

Taureans may find themselves salivating after simply reading the name of this cocktail. Indulge your characteristic sweet tooth (celestial bulls *love* desserts) and dazzle your friends with this easy-to-make treat. The Icy Vanilla Rum Malted Milkshake effortlessly combines rum, ice cream, and malted milk, serving up some dangerously delicious boozy cocktails. Taureans will love sipping on this creamy libation that evokes the classic imagery of a 1950s malt shop. But be careful! While this drink may appear innocent, its potency may surprise even the toughest bulls.

SERVES 1

¼ cup whole milk
⅓ cup vanilla ice cream
2 ounces light rum
1 teaspoon malted milk powder

Combine all ingredients in a blender filled with ice. Blend to create a smooth, creamy texture, and pour into a hurricane glass. Go crazy, Taurus darling—we won't tell.

Pink Lady

The Taurus sign is associated with femininity: celestial bulls capture the spirit of womanhood through their raw sensuality and luxe passions. The Pink Lady is the perfect cocktail for this earthy feminine sign. In fact, this beverage carries its own striking history. While the exact origins remain unknown, an early iteration of the drink is believed to have been invented in the early nineteenth century. At some point during the mid-1930s, the beverage became associated with "female tastes." That's right, cosmic goddesses, the Pink Lady was the first "girly" drink. Accordingly, the beverage was slammed by male cocktail critics who turned up their noses at its rosy hue. Despite the cocktail's delicious flavor, the beverage fell out of fashion. Let's reclaim this cocktail, Taurus darlings! The Pink Lady is an extremely tasty libation: not too sweet, with a dry, slightly tart flavor profile. Taureans will love sipping this delectable beverage while simultaneously celebrating their femininity and sticking it to "The Man."

SERVES 1

1½ ounces gin

4 dashes grenadine

1 egg white

Maraschino cherry, for garnish

Chill a martini glass in the freezer for five minutes. Combine all ingredients except garnish in a cocktail shaker filled with ice and shake vigorously. Strain into chilled cocktail glass. Garnish with a maraschino cherry and proudly celebrate this subversive treat!

Pomegranate Martini

Pomegranates are an ancient fruit rich in antioxidants and great for your heart health. And, when it comes to libations, pomegranates are also an absolutely delicious addition to your martini. Taureans will love the bold, tasty flavors; the tart and tangy notes of pomegranate juice make for a fun twist on the classic cocktail, while the rich crimson hue of the fruit juice creates a vibrant presentation. The Pomegranate Martini is a full sensory experience that epicurean Taureans will be sure to appreciate.

SERVES 1

3 ounces vodka
2 ounces pomegranate juice
5 pomegranate seeds, for garnish

Chill a martini glass in the freezer for five minutes. Combine vodka and pomegranate juice in a shaker filled with ice. Shake vigorously and strain into chilled martini glass. Sprinkle pomegranate seeds in the glass for garnish. The seeds will sink to the bottom and become boozy treats once you've finished your beverage—how fun!

Red Russian

Crimson tones are rumored to provoke even the most docile bulls, and Taureans will certainly charge for this delicious cocktail. The Red Russian is an eye-catching beverage that is named after its vibrant hue. Though there are many iterations of the Red Russian, the most simple (and tasty) variation combines cherry liqueur and vodka to create a deliciously refreshing treat. Taureans will love the refined elegance emphasized in the cherry liqueur's unique flavor profile. And, perhaps most important, the Red Russian's vibrant color is a great way to attract attention during happy hour, making it the perfect icebreaker to passionate flirting.

SERVES 1

2 ounces cherry liqueur
2 ounces vodka
Seasonal fruit, sliced, for garnish

Pour cherry liqueur and vodka into a rocks glass filled with ice and stir. Garnish with a seasonal fruit slice for added flair.

Red Velvet Shortcake

Sweet-toothed Taureans know that there's nothing quite like the taste of moist red velvet cake—capturing the richness of chocolate within a fluffy, crimson batter. This pastry's essence is perfectly emulated in the Red Velvet Shortcake cocktail. This mouthwatering beverage is like no other, combining vodka, cream soda, lemon juice, and strawberries to create a decadent delicacy. Taureans will adore this creative refreshment, which serves as a scrumptious treat for special occasions or after-dinner indulgences.

SERVES 1

3 fresh strawberries, hulled and divided
1½ ounces vodka

Splash lemon juice
2 ounces cream soda

Chill a highball glass in the freezer for five minutes. In a cocktail shaker, use a muddler or the base of a wooden spoon to muddle two strawberries. Fill shaker with ice and add vodka and lemon juice. Shake vigorously. Strain into chilled highball glass filled with fresh ice, and add cream soda. Decorate the glass with a fresh strawberry for a polished presentation.

Gemini

(MAY 21–JUNE 20): THE WORDSMITH

Gemini is the first air sign of the zodiac, and is symbolized by the twins. Though Gemini are often misrepresented as being two-faced, these fun-loving, sociable air signs rarely have ill intentions. In fact, the twins represent Gemini's distinctive versatility. Playful, spontaneous, and upbeat, Gemini are the social butterflies of the zodiac. These energetic twins can talk to anyone about anything, and are interested in exploring a range of topics and passions.

Intellectual Gemini are happiest when working on multiple projects simultaneously, as these restless air signs refuse to be confined to just one pathway. Gemini are ruled by Mercury (the planet that governs communication), and these fast talkers are renowned for their effortless self-expression. Gemini make excellent lyricists, poets, and writers, and attract friends and lovers through their bright charisma.

Gemini enjoy cocktails that spark conversation. These dynamic air signs love storytelling, and Gemini know that the perfect cocktail can provide a seamless segue into a riveting tale. Gemini will love exploring the mysterious origins of the Harvey Wallbanger and the clever etymology of the Caipiroska. Gemini find inspiration everywhere, and these twins are truly tantalized by unconventional libations. But astro-mixologists beware: playful Gemini should avoid sipping beverages that lack distinctive character. Though there's nothing wrong with simple mixed drinks, Gemini are inspired by beverages that facilitate intellectual amusement... as well as indulgence.

Aperol Spritz

This distinctive coral cocktail has been enjoyed in Italy for generations, widely regarded as the perfect midday refresher for beating the heat between meals. As the Aperol Spritz's popularity continues to expand, trendsetting Gemini are delighted to embrace this delicious aperitif. These eye-catching cocktails are also low in alcohol content, allowing even the thirstiest Gemini to enjoy a few glasses without losing their heads.

SERVES 1

4½ ounces prosecco
2½ ounces Aperol
Lime slice, seeded
1 ounce club soda

Pour prosecco into a Collins glass filled with ice. Pour in Aperol, and add lime slice and club soda. *Bellissimo!*

Bellini

Gemini are the "Energizer Bunnies" of the zodiac. Even after exhaustive partying, rambunctious Gemini wake up ready to roll. It's no surprise, then, that these vivacious air signs adore brunch, which provides the perfect platform to recap the previous night's events. The Bellini is the perfect cocktail to pair with Gemini's juicy chatter: this delicious beverage combines peach juice and prosecco for a tasty, chic morning treat.

SERVES 1

2 ounces peach juice
4 ounces prosecco

Pour peach juice into a champagne flute, and slowly add prosecco. When sharing the latest gossip, be sure to sip slowly, dear Gemini: you will *not* want to miss those juicy details!

Black Velvet

Gemini are all about duality (the sign is, after all, symbolized by the twins), making the Black Velvet the perfect cocktail for this dynamic air sign. The beverage is simple (half stout beer, half champagne), but the taste is complex. The Black Velvet effortlessly combines lowbrow and highbrow alcohols in a single glass, creating a uniquely fruity, creamy, and bubbly flavor profile. Gemini will enjoy the drink's distinctive flavor, as well as the sheer novelty. Serve up Black Velvets at your next party for the ultimate statement drink.

SERVES 1

4 ounces champagne
4 ounces chilled stout

Pour champagne into a pint glass, and slowly pour stout on top. Due to the alcohols' differing densities, the drink will have a layered effect. Good things (like Gemini) come in pairs—so relish this cocktail's dynamic coupling!

Blood and Sand

Blood and sand are two things you *definitely* don't want featured in your cocktail. But don't fear, Gemini dear, this classic concoction neither includes, nor tastes like, either ingredient. This historic cocktail's name was actually derived from a 1922 silent film of the same name. Though this cocktail's popularity waned throughout the twentieth century, a 1989 remake of the film (starring Sharon Stone) revitalized the beverage. In fact, one Los Angeles bar, the Dresden Room, has claimed this libation as its signature cocktail. Gemini will love this dynamic scotch-based refreshment, and will especially appreciate its eccentric silver-screen-linked history. After a few of these cocktails, you'll definitely be ready for your close-up.

SERVES 1

¾ ounce orange juice

¾ ounce sweet vermouth

¾ ounce cherry liqueur

¾ ounce scotch

Chill a cocktail glass in the freezer for five minutes. Combine all ingredients in a shaker filled with crushed ice, and shake vigorously for twenty seconds. Pour (with ice) into chilled cocktail glass for a stunningly textural presentation.

Boilermaker

Gemini are thrill-seekers, and these jovial, fun-loving air signs are not afraid to do whatever it takes to get the party bumpin'. While cocktail connoisseurs may turn up their noses at the Boilermaker, Gemini dive into this drink head first...literally. The directions are simple: drop a shot of whiskey into your favorite beer, and chug the concoction as fast as you possibly can. That's right, cosmic warriors, the Boilermaker is a no-frills, straightforward shooter best enjoyed among groups of like-minded rabble-rousers. Though the Boilermaker can also be spaced out as a shot of whiskey followed by a pint of beer, adrenaline junkie Gemini will love the playful activity. Bottoms up!

SERVES 1

8 ounces beer
1 ounce whiskey

Add beer to pint glass. Drop whiskey shot into glass and start chugging!

Caipiroska

Adventurous Gemini enjoy traveling, and a few sips of the Caipiroska will be sure to ignite this air sign's insatiable wanderlust. The Caipiroska is a clever adaptation of the Brazilian Caipirinha cocktail. This delicious beverage replaces cachaça (Brazil's signature liquor) with vodka, boasting a fresh, light flavor that highlights the cocktail's dominant citrus tang. The trick to making a flawless Caipiroska is impeccable muddling. Though this mixology technique takes practice, it's recommended that beginners engage their sense of smell while muddling: when the aroma of the fruits or herbs permeates the room, you'll know you've created a successfully muddled mash.

SERVES 1

1 lime, cut into 6 wedges
1 tablespoon granulated sugar

¼ cup vodka

Using a muddler, or the handle of a wooden spoon, lightly muddle lime and sugar in a cocktail shaker to release juice (press the limes firmly enough to release the juice, but keep the fruit's meat on the peel). When finished, stir mash until sugar completely dissolves. Add vodka. Fill an old-fashioned glass halfway with crushed ice, and pour vodka mixture over ice. Pour the entire mixture (including the fresh ice) back into the shaker to mix. After a few gentle shakes, return concoction to old-fashioned glass.

Frozen Banana Daiquiri

With Gemini kicking off the summer season, these air signs prepare for the warm weather (and their birthdays!) by serving up delicious tropical favorites. The Frozen Banana Daiquiri is a classic frosty cocktail that always heralds a fabulous time, making it the ideal libation for fun-loving Gemini. Though the Frozen Banana Daiquiri shares a name with the traditional Daiquiri cocktail, the two beverages are quite different. The Frozen Banana Daiquiri is blended (not stirred) and includes bananas and coconut milk in addition to the classic rum and lime ingredients. This delectably frosty beverage is a classic vacation essential, and whether Gemini plan to spend the summer relaxing by the beach or party-hopping with their friends, they will love sipping this decadent mixer.

SERVES 2

½ cup coconut milk
¼ cup granulated sugar
2 ounces light rum

1 large banana, sliced
1 ounce lime juice
2 maraschino cherries, for garnish

Chill two hurricane glasses in the freezer for five minutes. Combine all ingredients except garnish in blender and blend until smooth. Pour into chilled hurricane glasses, and garnish each with a maraschino cherry.

Fuzzy Navel

Gemini are celebrated for their lighthearted nature, and these playful air signs enjoy beverages that showcase their wacky dispositions. There are few drinks that are sillier—both in name and association—than the Fuzzy Navel, making this vibrant beverage the perfect Gemini libation. This cheerful cocktail was invented by esteemed mixologist Ray Foley in 1985, and immediately became an overnight sensation. In fact, this cocktail's quick rise to stardom has made it synonymous with 1980s culture, and it is now widely regarded as a quintessential "throwback" beverage. Who knows, Gemini, after a few sips of this iconic peach-schnapps-and-orange-juice concoction, you may end up busting out some retro shoulder pads and neon leg warmers yourself.

SERVES 1

3 ounces peach schnapps

3 ounces orange juice

Combine all ingredients in a highball glass filled with ice and stir. Totally tubular!

Gin Fizz

Gemini are the social butterflies of the zodiac, and these playful air signs are often found buzzing between parties and social gatherings. Gemini will love taking their buoyancy to the next level with Gin Fizz cocktails. These frothy, bubbly elixirs are made by combining gin, club soda, lemon juice, egg whites, and simple syrup, creating a light, citrusy flavor that highlights the gin's herbal qualities. Though the ingredients are fairly straightforward, the real trick to making a perfect Gin Fizz is all in the wrist. The Gin Fizz's characteristic foam is achieved by vigorous—and we mean *vigorous*—shaking. That's right, Gemini darling, you'll finally have an excuse to bounce off the walls!

SERVES 1

1 ounce club soda
1 ounce gin
1 ounce lemon juice

¾ ounce simple syrup
1 egg white

Pour club soda into a Collins glass and set aside. Combine remaining ingredients in a shaker. Shake the mixture (with all your might!) for ten seconds. Add three ice cubes to shaker and—again—shake vigorously (really put your heart into it, Gemini!). Double-strain into prepared Collins glass, and take a big swig to commemorate a job well done.

Harvey Wallbanger

Gemini, represented by the twins, are the social chameleons of the zodiac. These eccentric air signs seamlessly adapt to their environments, using different aspects of their personality to match situation requirements. The Harvey Wallbanger is an equally mutable cocktail, making it the perfect Gemini beverage. This simple drink combines vodka, orange juice, and a Galliano float to create a dynamic herbal and citrusy flavor. While the ingredients are straightforward, its legend is a bit more hazy: though the cocktail is believed to date back to the 1950s, its popularity peaked during the 1970s disco era, when several different bartenders, restaurants, and companies took credit for inventing this tangy treat. Though we may never know the *true* origins of the Harvey Wallbanger, its elusive history and accessible ingredients make it an extremely versatile beverage that Gemini are sure to enjoy.

SERVES 1

1½ ounces vodka

4 ounces orange juice

½ ounce Galliano

Orange slice, seeded, for garnish

Pour vodka and orange juice into a Collins glass filled with ice, and float Galliano to the top by pouring it slowly over the back of a bar spoon. Garnish with an orange slice and voilà: a perfectly retro treat!

Key Lime Martini

The key lime flavor is tangy, refreshing...and absolutely perfect in cocktail form. Gemini will love bringing this classic dessert to life with a tasty Key Lime Martini. This beverage seamlessly blends sweet and sour by combining notes of vanilla with fresh citrus. This well-balanced cocktail can be enjoyed during happy hour or as a late-night treat, making it the ideal accessory for all occasions. The Key Lime Martini is also super easy to make, and since they're so sinfully delicious, it may be impossible for any sweet-toothed Gemini to enjoy just one!

SERVES 1

2 ounces vanilla vodka
1 ounce vanilla liqueur
1 ounce lime juice
1 ounce pineapple juice
Lime wedge, for garnish

Chill a martini glass in the freezer for five minutes. Combine all ingredients except garnish in a shaker filled with ice. Shake vigorously and strain into chilled martini glass. Garnish with lime wedge for extra pizzazz.

Kryptonite Cocktail

Superman *must* have been a Gemini. By day he was a quirky, mild-mannered journalist named Clark Kent...but by night, he was a crime-fighting superhero with extraordinary powers. Gemini will relate to Superman's plight: just as Superman was constantly juggling his alter egos, Gemini are constantly multitasking their many passions. Deepen your superhero bond with the Kryptonite Cocktail. This potent libation features vodka, olive juice, and garlic, and is bound to deliver an instant pick-me-up. But a word to the wise, darling Gemini: if you plan to enjoy this powerful treat on a date, you may want to bring a few mints. Don't let this pungent beverage be your tragic downfall!

SERVES 1

2 ounces vodka
1 clove garlic, minced
Splash olive juice

3 cocktail onions, for garnish
Green olive, for garnish

Chill a martini glass in the freezer for five minutes. Combine all ingredients except garnishes in a shaker filled with ice. Shake vigorously and strain into chilled martini glass. Thread cocktail onions and olive onto a toothpick, and balance the garnish atop your cocktail. Enjoy!

Monkey Gland

Though this drink's name isn't exactly appetizing, the Monkey Gland is actually a surprisingly delicious cocktail that boasts an *extremely* juicy history. This oddly titled beverage originated in Paris in the 1920s, and combines gin, orange juice, grenadine, and absinthe to create a uniquely zesty, herbal flavor. But what's even more compelling than the cocktail's ingredients is the story behind its bizarre name. Throughout the 1920s and 1930s, avant-garde surgeon Dr. Serge Voronoff experimented with grafting monkey tissue to humans as a way of increasing longevity. Yes, you read that correctly. What's even crazier is that Voronoff's procedures were considered in vogue, and were in exceptionally high demand. Weirded out yet? Of course you're not, Gemini darling! Gemini love unusual factoids, making the iconic Monkey Gland the perfect cocktail for this curious sign.

SERVES 1

Dash absinthe
2 ounces gin
1 ounce orange juice

¼ ounce grenadine
Orange slice, seeded, for garnish

Chill a cocktail glass in the freezer for five minutes. Swirl dash of absinthe in chilled cocktail glass to coat it, then discard excess liqueur. Pour remaining ingredients (except garnish) into a cocktail shaker filled with ice and shake well. Strain into prepared cocktail glass and garnish with an orange slice. Additional monkey decorations are optional.

Singapore Sling

Gemini are storytellers and love cocktails that carry history, making the Singapore Sling a perfectly suited cocktail for these curious twins. The Singapore Sling was invented in 1915 by bartender Ngiam Tong Boon at the Raffles Hotel in Singapore. The crafty bartender had a clear goal: he wanted to make an innocuous-looking beverage that (though containing an assortment of alcohol) resembled fruit juice, allowing women to enjoy the cocktail in public. Ngiam experimented with different combinations and measurements, finally settling on a carefully proportioned set of ingredients that gave the drink its signature rosy hue. And just like that, the Singapore Sling was born. Gemini will appreciate this iconic beverage that not only tastes delicious, but also prompts some pretty fascinating happy hour chatter.

SERVES 1

1½ ounces gin
1 ounce Bénédictine
1 ounce lime juice
¼ ounce simple syrup

2 ounces club soda
½ ounce cherry brandy
Lemon slice, seeded, for garnish
Maraschino cherry, for garnish

Pour gin, Bénédictine, lime juice, and simple syrup into a cocktail shaker filled with ice. Shake well and strain into a highball glass over fresh ice. Pour in club soda, and float cherry brandy to the top by pouring it over the back of a bar spoon (this takes practice!). Garnish with lemon slice and cherry for a classic presentation.

Spiked Cider

Playful Gemini always know how to get the party going. These mischievous twins can turn even the drabbest affair into a complete rager, so it's no surprise that this air sign loves preparing (and enjoying!) Spiked Cider. Even without the alcohol, cider is a scrumptious hot beverage that combines spicy cinnamon and cloves with apples and oranges, creating a unique, zesty flavor perfect for cool fall nights. These rich notes are further enhanced when bourbon is added to the mix, resulting in a superb boozy concoction. Spiked Cider is the perfect addition to any social gathering, and Gemini will love playing host while serving up this deliciously autumnal cocktail.

SERVES 1

4 cups apple cider
1 tablespoon orange juice
2 cinnamon sticks, divided
3 whole cloves

1 star anise
2 ounces bourbon
Orange slice, seeded, for garnish

Place apple cider, orange juice, one cinnamon stick, cloves, and star anise in a small pot over high heat and bring to a boil. Lower to a simmer for five to ten minutes. Remove from heat and strain into a pitcher. In a rocks glass, combine cider mixture with bourbon. Garnish with an orange slice, remaining cinnamon stick, and a festive spirit.

Summer Shandy

Summer Shandies are the quintessential beer-based cocktail. In fact, these deliciously tangy and refreshing seasonal beverages are so superb that many beer companies now sell this concoction as a prepackaged mixture. Wise Gemini know, however, that there's *nothing* better than a homemade Summer Shandy. These warm-weather treats—equal parts beer and lemonade—can be easily prepared on the go, and are essential companions for barbecues, picnics, and beach adventures. Gemini who are extra inspired by playing host can offer a variety of beers and lemonade types, encouraging guests to experiment with the different flavor profiles to make their own "Signature Shandy."

SERVES 1

6 ounces beer
6 ounces lemonade
Lemon slice, seeded, for garnish

Pour beer into pint glass, then add lemonade. Garnish with a lemon slice for timeless summer twist.

Cancer

(JUNE 21–JULY 22): THE FEELER

Cancers are symbolized by the crab, and, like this armored crustacean, those born under the Cancer constellation often protect their soft interior with a hard outer shell. Cancers need to feel fully comfortable before opening up to new friends or partners, so trust and loyalty are critical for these sweet water signs. Cancer is ruled by the moon—the celestial body that governs our emotions and security. Accordingly, Cancers enjoy cultivating nurturing and supportive environments built on love, dedication, and mutual respect. Not vibing with Cancer's domestic sensibilities? That could be a problem. Cancers are also highly intuitive, and when they sense judgment, these crabs won't hesitate to pinch you with their claws. Ouch!

Cancers are very affected by climate, so these delicate crabs enjoy cocktails that reflect their environmental surroundings. During the colder months, Cancers will enjoy the rich flavors of Eggnog, Hot Buttered Rum, and the Godmother. When the weather heats up, however, Cancers will vibe on tropical favorites such as Sex on the Beach and Boozy Strawberry Lemonade. When mixing up a concoction for a Cancer friend or lover, be mindful of Cancer's unique tastes and interests: if you can't remember Cancer's unique preferences, don't be afraid to ask!

Americano

Did you know that the United States of America is a Cancer? That's right, sweet crabs, zodiac signs aren't just ascribed to people. In the astrological community, cosmic insight is also bestowed upon major historical events. The Declaration of Independence was ratified on July 4, thus birthing the United States of America. If you think about it, the USA is *super* Cancerian: it's a country that tries to appear tough, despite being founded on very compassionate, egalitarian principles. Celebrate this Cancerian holiday with a classical Americano. This spirit-forward cocktail combines Campari, vermouth, and club soda to create a totally tasty beverage that will be sure to usher in fireworks.

SERVES 1

1½ ounces Campari
1½ ounces sweet vermouth

3 ounces club soda
Lemon twist, for garnish

Pour Campari and vermouth into an old-fashioned glass filled with ice, and add club soda. Garnish with a lemon twist, and prepare to let freedom ring!

Beachbum's Own

Sure, tiki drinks may be a little kitschy, Cancer darling, but you're going to absolutely love Beachbum's Own. This lesser-known tropical cocktail is a well-balanced mixture of deliciously fruity favorites (orange juice, pineapple juice, lemon juice, and passion fruit puree) and potent booze (rum and Licor 43—a Spanish liqueur known for its dynamic herbal infusion). This cocktail is not as sweet as other tiki classics, making it much more palatable (and less likely to induce a hangover). Cancers will enjoy the unique and bold flavor combinations of Beachbum's Own, but be careful! Though this beverage hides its potency, it packs a mean punch. Sip slowly, or you may end up swept out to sea.

SERVES 1

3 ounces light rum

¾ ounce Licor 43

¾ ounce unsweetened pineapple juice

¾ ounce orange juice

¾ ounce lemon juice

¾ ounce passion fruit puree

Cocktail umbrella, for garnish

Combine all ingredients except garnish in a shaker filled with crushed ice and shake vigorously. Pour unstrained mixture into a tiki mug, garnish with cocktail umbrella, and get ready for a whole lot of fun!

Boozy Strawberry Lemonade

For Cancers who prefer the pool to the ocean, Boozy Strawberry Lemonade cocktails are the perfect sunbathing companion. Cancers will love preparing, sipping, and sharing this stunning summertime favorite. Sporting a playful rosy hue, this cocktail is the ideal accessory to warm-weather fashion, and looks fabulous featured in any impromptu photo shoot...including selfies. Boozy Strawberry Lemonade combines the zesty citrus notes of lemonade and rosé with the refreshing, sweet flavor of fresh strawberries. This beverage is so delicious, it will be impossible to have just one!

SERVES 6

1 (25-ounce) bottle dry
    sparkling rosé
1 cup vodka
12 ounces lemonade

½ cup club soda
2 cups strawberries, hulled and
    sliced
3 small lemons, sliced

Combine all ingredients in a large pitcher. Stir and refrigerate until chilled (one hour minimum, though flavors will marinate best overnight).

Dirty Shirley

The Dirty Shirley is the perfect cocktail for Cancers, capturing both the nice and naughty sides of these celestial crabs. These clever concoctions spice up your favorite childhood mocktail (the Shirley Temple) by adding a healthy dose of cherry vodka to the already tasty beverage. Though the original nonalcoholic variation was designed to serve children dining with their families, it was simply too delicious not to spike. Nostalgic Cancers will love sipping this sweet libation that will be sure to inspire a stroll down memory lane.

SERVES 1

2 ounces cherry vodka
4 ounces ginger ale
1 teaspoon grenadine
Lime wedge, for garnish
Maraschino cherry, for garnish

Fill a Collins glass with ice and add cherry vodka, followed by ginger ale. Slowly pour grenadine along the side of the glass so it sinks to the bottom. Stir, then garnish with a lime wedge and, of course, the iconic maraschino cherry!

Eggnog

Cancers are among the most sensitive and nurturing signs of the zodiac. In the winter, these sweet water signs enjoy serving cheerful refreshments that embody the celestial crab's warmhearted nature. Eggnog is the ideal seasonal cocktail for homey Cancers. This classic holiday beverage has been enjoyed for centuries, with early iterations of the creamy cocktail dating back to the 1700s. It's no surprise that this holiday drink's popularity has persisted over the years: its well-balanced combination of brandy, vanilla, milk, and (of course) eggs perfectly captures the warm embrace of home.

SERVES 4

6 eggs, separated
½ cup granulated sugar, divided
2 tablespoons nutmeg
¼ teaspoon kosher salt

2 teaspoons vanilla
   extract
2 cups brandy
1 cup whole milk

Beat egg yolks, ¼ cup sugar, nutmeg, salt, and vanilla together until mixture is very thick with a light-yellow hue. Slowly add brandy and milk, continuing to beat the ingredients. Cover and chill in the refrigerator overnight. Before serving, beat together egg whites and remaining sugar. Continue whipping until mixture has achieved a fluffy, meringue-like consistency. Slowly pour over chilled brandy mixture and stir to combine. Serve Eggnog in an Irish coffee glass, and enjoy this decadent treat made with love!

Frozen Beer Margarita

Cancers love to play host, and Frozen Beer Margaritas are the perfect companion for summertime hangs. These potent libations will spice up any event, and the unusual ingredients will be sure to dazzle your guests. Frozen Beer Margaritas combine tequila, triple sec, orange juice, and Mexican beer, creating a distinctive tangy flavor and subtle sparkle. This cocktail is also super easy to prepare, which will definitely come in handy when your guests demand seconds...and even thirds! Frozen Beer Margaritas are an instant sensation, so be sure to have extra ingredients ready for additional rounds.

SERVES 1

1 cup lime juice, frozen
1¼ cups orange juice, frozen
1¾ cups gold tequila

1½ cups triple sec
1 (12-ounce) bottle Mexican beer
Lime slice, seeded, for garnish

Combine all ingredients except beer and garnish in a blender. Blend until smooth. Transfer mixture into a pitcher and add beer, stirring gently to combine flavors. Garnish the rim with lime slice, and get ready to party!

Godmother

Since Cancers are regarded as the mothers of the zodiac, the classic Godmother may very well be this sign's signature cocktail. This vodka-based beverage is the softer variation of the scotch-heavy Godfather (a tasty classic you'll find under Cancer's opposite sign, Capricorn, which represents the father of the zodiac). The Godmother is a simple and great-tasting beverage that highlights the rich almond flavor of amaretto. This easy-to-drink cocktail is the perfect happy hour beverage, but can also be enjoyed as a classy nightcap. No matter when you choose to enjoy this sophisticated drink, you'll be sure to savor each sip.

SERVES 1

1½ ounces vodka
1½ ounces amaretto

Add all ingredients to an old-fashioned glass filled with ice. Sip slowly to enjoy the rich, enveloping aromas that effortlessly mirror Cancer's nurturing sensibilities.

Hot Buttered Rum

Cancer's moods are very much influenced by their environments, so it's critically important that these sensitive crabs enjoy cocktails crafted specifically for each season. Since Cancers are born during the summer, these sweet water signs need to stay warm during the chilly winter months. Hot Buttered Rum is the perfect beverage to enjoy on the frostiest nights. This delicious cocktail dates back to the colonial era, when it was used to warm up early American settlers. Hot Buttered Rum combines heated rum with an extraordinary blend of spices (cinnamon, nutmeg, and allspice) that is guaranteed to thaw even the most frozen Cancers.

SERVES 1

1 teaspoon soft butter
1 teaspoon brown sugar
Dash ground cinnamon
Dash ground nutmeg

Dash allspice
Splash vanilla extract
2 ounces dark rum
5 ounces hot water

Combine butter, sugar, spices, and vanilla extract in the bottom of an Irish coffee glass. Carefully muddle ingredients using a muddler or the base of a wooden spoon. Pour in rum, followed by hot water. Stir to combine. Fireplace and cozy blanket optional!

Mother's Little Helper

In traditional astrology, Cancer represents the mother. Though this sign does have a masculine side as well (in tarot, Cancer is symbolized by the Chariot card, which depicts an athletic young man riding off to battle), Cancer's nurturing, domestic, and protective spirit reflects maternal ideals. But Cancers know that it's not easy taking care of everyone all the time, and these celestial crabs definitely deserve a pick-me-up every now and then. Mother's Little Helper is a perfect cocktail for stressed Cancers. This delicious hot beverage consists of rum, apple cider, and clove, creating a soothing sensation that is guaranteed to relieve even the most aggravating headaches.

SERVES 1

3 ounces apple cider

2 ounces dark rum

⅛ teaspoon ground cloves

Combine all ingredients in an Irish coffee glass, stir, and microwave for a quick sixty seconds for instant gratification. Don't worry—we won't tell.

Navy Grog

Cancers are at home by the water, so naturally they will love sipping on this maritime classic. Though now regarded as a tiki bar favorite, the Navy Grog has much older roots. The word "grog" is an old term used to define a variety of alcoholic drinks. Grogs were much grittier than our present-day cocktails: sailors drank grogs both to conceal the rancid taste of stagnant water and to fight off terminal seaborne illnesses during the eighteenth century. How appetizing. During the tiki craze of the 1950s, the Navy Grog transformed into the delicious, rum-based beverage enjoyed today.

SERVES 1

1 ounce white rum
1 ounce Demerara rum
1 ounce dark rum
1 ounce honey syrup
¾ ounce lime juice

¾ ounce white grapefruit juice
5 ounces club soda
Orange slice, seeded, for garnish
Maraschino cherry,
    for garnish

Pour rums, syrup, and juices into a cocktail shaker filled with ice. Shake well, and strain into a Collins glass filled with fresh ice. Add club soda and garnish with orange slice and maraschino cherry. Ahoy!

Sex on the Beach

Sure, Cancers have a tough exterior. These celestial crabs are extremely self-protective, and because they are usually private about their personal lives, they're not often thought of as a hyper-sensual sign. The truth is, however, that though these crabs may first appear shy, they really let loose as soon as they're comfortable. Despite popular opinion, Cancers are extremely passionate water signs, making Sex on the Beach the perfect secret weapon. This iconic fruity beverage combines vodka, peach schnapps, orange juice, and cranberry juice to create a super-sippable cocktail perfect for tropical trysts. Let's face it, Cancer darling, there's nowhere you would rather get down than by the shore.

SERVES 1

1½ ounces vodka
1½ ounces orange juice
1½ ounces cranberry juice

½ ounce peach schnapps
Orange slice, seeded, for garnish

Add all ingredients except garnish to a shaker filled with ice. Shake vigorously, and strain into a highball glass filled with fresh ice. Garnish with orange slice. Clothing optional.

Sidewalker

Crustaceans move sideways, always walking at an angle. Similarly, Cancers tend to avoid direct confrontation by skirting difficult conversations. One cocktail these clever crabs will be sure to approach head on, however, is the tasty Sidewalker. Appropriately named to match Cancer's signature glide, the Sidewalker is a delicious beer-based cocktail that includes apple brandy, lemon juice, and maple syrup. The Sidewalker's dynamic flavor profile is bold, tangy, and buoyant, featuring rich autumnal notes perfect for a picnic in the early fall. Cancers will love serving up this modern cocktail that is guaranteed to be an instant classic.

SERVES 4

½ cup apple brandy

¾ cup lemon juice

½ cup pure maple syrup

2 cups wheat beer

½ cup club soda

8 lemon wedges

Pour apple brandy, lemon juice, and maple syrup into a large pitcher and stir until syrup is blended. Add beer, club soda, and lemon wedges. Stir lightly to combine, and pour into four highball glasses.

Snuggler

Community is super important to these gentle water signs, and during the frigid winter, these celestial crabs like to stay cozy surrounded by their friends, family, and lovers. Cancers will love to get toasty with the Snuggler. This perfectly titled beverage combines peppermint schnapps, hot chocolate, and whipped cream for an easy-to-make, delicious dessert treat. The peppermint flavor adds a dynamic boozy sweetness, while the steaming hot cocoa will feel like a warm embrace. This comforting cocktail is the ideal elixir during the colder months, and Cancers will enjoy serving up this homey drink for their closest companions.

SERVES 1

1 packet instant hot chocolate
1 cup steaming hot water

1 ounce peppermint schnapps
Whipped cream, for garnish

Prepare hot chocolate by adding packet of instant hot chocolate to a mug of hot water. Add peppermint schnapps. Garnish with whipped cream, fuzzy socks, and a soft blanket.

Tequila Lime Spritzer

Cancers are ruled by the moon, and like this quick-moving celestial body, their moods are constantly changing. Though they are known for their domestic and homey dispositions, these celestial crabs also have a bit of a wild side. Embrace your mischievous nature with the Tequila Lime Spritzer, the perfect summer cocktail for Cancers. This delicious beverage highlights tequila's distinctive flavor through a perfect combination of lime juice, club soda, and salt. Though the ingredients are similar to those of the classic Margarita, this simple concoction is much easier to prepare, making it the ideal accessory for a warm-weather hang.

SERVES 1

1 lime, halved and divided
Sea salt
1 ounce silver tequila
Club soda

Flavor the rim of a Collins glass by first rubbing half a lime along the rim and dipping the top of the glass into a bowl of sea salt. Fill the glass with ice and squeeze in juice from second half of lime. Pour in tequila, and fill the rest of the glass with club soda. Enjoy, sweet Cancer!

White Sangria

When entertaining guests, Cancers love channeling their inner Julia Child. These water signs enjoy showcasing their domestic sensibilities, focusing on every detail to create the perfect ambiance for every occasion. White Sangria is a terrific party drink that domestic Cancers will adore. This classic Iberian beverage dates back to the 1700s, and although red wine is the more traditional base for Sangria (*sangre* means "blood" in Spanish), the white wine variation has become widely popular in recent years. This light and refreshing concoction features dynamic citrus flavors and enchanting bubbles, perfectly complementing the wine's intrinsic tangy notes.

SERVES 6

¼ cup brandy
2 tablespoons granulated sugar
1 (25-ounce) bottle dry white wine
1 small lemon, sliced and seeded

1 lime, sliced and seeded
1 cup peaches, sliced
1 cup strawberries, hulled and sliced
12 ounces club soda

Combine brandy and sugar in a pitcher until sugar is totally dissolved. Fill pitcher with ice and add remaining ingredients, stirring gently to combine. Pour into white wine glasses with fresh ice. *¡Delicioso!*

Yaka Hula Hickey Dula

Represented by the crab, Cancers love spending time by the shore. In fact, these celestial crustaceans are most deeply connected to their innate psychic abilities when near water. The Yaka Hula Hickey Dula is the perfect tropical cocktail for Cancers, effortlessly capturing the mellow beachside vibes that Cancers so deeply crave. This fruity concoction was invented in the early twentieth century and takes its name from a popular Hawaiian love song of the same title. The Yaka Hula Hickey Dula's simple ingredients (rum, vermouth, and pineapple juice) create a classic flavor profile that is a well-balanced mix of sweet and sour. Cancers will love this timeless island favorite that brings out the true spirit of paradise.

SERVES 1

1½ ounces dark rum
1½ ounces dry vermouth
1½ ounces pineapple juice

Chill a cocktail glass in the freezer for five minutes. Combine all ingredients in a cocktail shaker filled with ice. Shake vigorously and strain into chilled cocktail glass. Don't forget your grass skirt and coconuts: it's time to hula!

Leo

(JULY 23–AUGUST 22): THE SUPERSTAR

Those born under the Leo constellation are always ready for their close-up. Leos are ruled by the sun, and these fire signs definitely envision themselves as the center of the universe. Celestial lions love classic, old-Hollywood-style romances, including grandiose displays of affection and paparazzi-worthy drama. Leos are natural leaders and excel in creative pursuits—especially those with a theatrical flair. Though performative lions worship the spotlight, they are also extremely devoted to their friends, family, and lovers. Lions travel in prides, and these wild felines build community through their magnetic personalities and warmhearted dispositions.

Regal Leos enjoy beverages that look as good as they taste. Since lions love to entertain, an eye-catching cocktail is the ideal accessory for holding court at a bar or party. Zesty, bold, and sparkling beverages perfectly complement Leos' vivacious spirit.

However, *never* serve your Leo friend or lover a carelessly thrown together concoction. Leos put their heart into everything they touch, so these fiery lions are insulted by poorly prepared cocktails. Best to avoid the drama and stick to bold beverages that will make them purr. From the chic Cosmopolitan to the playful Piña Colada, Leos know that the right cocktail is the ultimate statement piece.

Bijou

Enchanté, Bijou! Leos will adore this classy cocktail that boasts a rich (and *très chic*) history. This time-honored beverage dates back to the late 1800s and is considered one of the earliest mixology creations. The Bijou, which means "jewel" in French, is named after its three dazzling ingredients: gin (representing diamonds), vermouth (representing rubies), and Chartreuse (representing emeralds). Regal Leos will love this cocktail's enchanting origins, as well as its sophisticated flavors. A few sips of Bijou, and you'll instantly be transported back to early twentieth-century Paris—every celestial lion's dream come true!

SERVES 1

1 ounce gin
1 ounce sweet vermouth
1 ounce Chartreuse

Dash orange bitters
Lemon twist, for garnish

Chill a martini glass in the freezer for five minutes. Combine all ingredients except garnish in a mixing glass filled with ice. Stir gently and strain into chilled cocktail glass. Garnish with lemon twist. The luxe life comes naturally to you, regal Leo, so don't be surprised if this bedazzling blend quickly becomes your go-to cocktail.

Breakfast Martini

Leos know that breakfast is the most important meal of the day—so make it count with a delicious Breakfast Martini! Regal lions are always seeking new opportunities to shine, so start glowing before noon by kicking off your day with this tasty, indulgent treat. This classic beverage is prepared with gin, lemon juice, simple syrup, and orange marmalade. The marmalade creates an alluring citrusy flavor, a distinctive texture, and the perfect morning-after solution for your most dramatic benders. Leos will love this refreshing morning pick-me-up that serves as the perfect brunch companion.

SERVES 1

1½ ounces gin
¾ ounce lemon juice
½ ounce simple syrup

2 teaspoons orange
  marmalade
Lemon twist, for garnish

Combine all ingredients except garnish in a cocktail shaker filled with ice. Shake, and strain into a cocktail glass, garnishing with lemon peel. For a balanced meal, serve with a side of warm buttered toast.

Cosmopolitan

Glamour is nonnegotiable for extravagant lions. And, when it comes to cocktails, nothing is as elegant as the rose-hued Cosmopolitan. Like Leos, Cosmopolitans (informally known as "Cosmos") are colorful, buoyant, and iconic. This classic beverage originated in the early twentieth century and became ubiquitous in the 1990s, thanks to the stylish BFFs on HBO's *Sex and the City*. The eye-catching Cosmopolitan is often served in a martini glass and garnished with a citrus slice or wedge for an added dose of drama. Extravagant Leos will feel extra luxe when sipping these distinctive libations, and will relish the charm...that also packs a punch.

SERVES 1

1½ ounces citrus vodka
½ ounce lime juice
1 ounce triple sec

Dash cranberry juice
Lime slice, seeded,
    for garnish

Chill a cocktail glass in the freezer for five minutes. Combine vodka, lime juice, triple sec, and cranberry juice in a cocktail shaker filled with ice. Shake until chilled. Strain into chilled cocktail glass, and garnish with a lime slice for an extra fabulous presentation. At last, a cocktail as magnificent as you are, lovely Leo! Cheers!

Coupe de Ville

While Leos may find most beer cocktail recipes a bit gauche, these glamorous lions will adore the Coupe de Ville. Named after the effortlessly cool top-down town cars of the 1960s, this delicious beer-based Margarita will make any celestial Leo feel like the hippest wildcat in town. This sophisticated beverage fluidly combines añejo tequila, lime juice, orange juice, orange liqueur, and Mexican beer to create a dynamic flavor profile. The Coupe de Ville is smooth, tangy, and sparkling, and Leos will love its eye-catching orange hue.

SERVES 1

1 ounce añejo tequila
1 ounce lime juice
1 ounce orange juice

½ ounce orange liqueur
1 (12-ounce) bottle light
    Mexican beer

Chill a pint glass in the freezer for five minutes. Combine all ingredients except beer in a mixing glass filled with ice and stir to combine. Transfer to chilled pint glass and gently stir in beer.

Fortune Teller

Did you know that the iconic Miss Cleo was a Leo (born August 12, 1962)? Though psychic abilities are traditionally associated with water signs, who else could possibly play the role of a fortune teller better than a Leo? These celestial lions are the most theatrical sign of the zodiac, and their larger-than-life personalities are perfectly suited for dramatics performed over a glowing crystal ball. The Fortune Teller cocktail is the ideal accessory for aspiring Leo starlets. This spellbinding beverage mixes tequila with sherry and cherry liqueur, creating a completely enchanting elixir. Though it can't promise clairvoyance, after a few sips, Leos will surely be glowing.

SERVES 1

1½ ounces silver tequila

1 ounce sherry

1 ounce cherry liqueur

Lemon peel, for garnish

Combine all ingredients except garnish in a mixing glass filled with ice. Stir and strain into a rocks glass with one large ice cube. Add lemon peel to garnish—and a fog machine for an extra-dramatic effect.

Harrogate Nights

Imagine yourself in an aristocratic spa town in the English countryside: it's a warm summer evening, and the sun is just beginning to set. You can feel the night's electricity building, and you know there is magic ahead. If this striking scenario is at all intriguing, darling Leo, you'll be thrilled to try the classic cocktail Harrogate Nights. This colorful, vodka-based concoction combines peach schnapps, pineapple juice, and melon liqueur. Though its specific origins remain unknown, this beverage's popularity grew in the affluent town of Harrogate, England, giving it its name. Imaginative Leos will love the intriguing fruit flavors of Harrogate Nights, as well as its sophisticated backstory.

SERVES 1

1 ounce melon liqueur
1 ounce vodka
1 ounce peach schnapps

4 ounces pineapple juice
Orange twist, for garnish

Fill a highball glass with ice. Slowly pour melon liqueur so it fills the bottom of the glass. Add vodka, peach schnapps, and pineapple juice. Garnish with an orange twist.

Liquid Diamond

Leos know that we are living in a material world (Madonna is, in fact, a fellow lioness), and that diamonds are not actually forever. But that doesn't mean Leos don't want to sparkle! The Liquid Diamond cocktail is the perfect treat for extravagant lions. The zesty combination of gin, lime juice, and white cranberry juice is poured over a rocks glass overflowing with crushed ice, creating a stunning, twinkling effect that reflects this beverage's plush name.

SERVES 1

2 ounces gin
1 ounce lime juice
1 ounce white cranberry juice

Combine all ingredients in a shaker filled with ice. Shake vigorously and strain into a rocks glass over crushed ice. Stir until the glass is frosted on the outside, and top with more crushed ice to form an ice dome. How fancy!

Liquid Sunshine

Leos are playful, creative, and expressive, and enjoy cocktails that reflect their cheerful values. These exuberant fire signs will love the Liquid Sunshine cocktail, a bright and tasty beverage with tropical citrus flavors. This boozy beauty also boasts a stunning orange hue that resembles the sun's warm glow. Leos will adore this lighthearted beverage that effortlessly mirrors the sign's own shining traits.

SERVES 1

3 ounces light rum
1½ ounces peach schnapps
⅓ cup orange juice
⅓ cup pineapple juice

Splash grenadine
Orange slice, seeded, for garnish
Pineapple cube, for garnish
Maraschino cherry, for garnish

Fill a highball glass with ice. Pour in rum and peach schnapps, followed by orange juice and pineapple juice. Stir gently, and carefully drizzle grenadine over the edge of the glass, allowing liquid to sink to the bottom. For an added dose of playfulness, garnish with orange slice, pineapple cube, and maraschino cherry.

Piña Colada

Though Leos do *not* enjoy getting caught in the rain (it totally ruins their lions' manes!), they do adore Piña Coladas. These blended cocktails are the quintessential tropical treat, deliciously mixing coconut's creamy texture with pineapple's tangy flavor. The Piña Colada also boasts a fascinating history. The earliest iteration of the beverage is believed to have been invented in the early 1800s by a Puerto Rican pirate named Robert Cofresí, who made the tasty concoction to boost his crew's morale. Though the recipe faded into obscurity after Cofresí's death in 1825, it was revived over one hundred years later by a Puerto Rican bartender named Ramón "Monchito" Marrero in the mid-1950s. Monchito perfected this mouthwatering cocktail, creating the modern Piña Colada. The Piña Colada is now the official national drink of Puerto Rico, and remains one of the most popular island cocktails. With such a delicious flavor and equally juicy history, it's no wonder that Leos love this tropical treat.

SERVES 1

2 ounces coconut milk
2 ounces pineapple juice
1½ ounces light rum

Maraschino cherry, for garnish
Pineapple wedge, for garnish

Combine all ingredients except garnishes in a shaker filled with ice and shake vigorously. Once mixture is smooth and creamy, strain into a hurricane glass filled with fresh ice. And don't forget: no Piña Colada is complete without the signature maraschino cherry and pineapple wedge garnishes!

Sake Champagne Mojito

Is your passport ready? Jet-setting Leos will adore the spirited Sake Champagne Mojito. This delicious cocktail is a flavor excursion from around the world, merging the signature beverages of Japan, France, and Cuba in one seamless libation. Sake's smooth texture perfectly enhances champagne's sparkling buoyancy, while the muddled mint leaves create a refreshingly aromatic punch that brings it all together. This exceptional cocktail is worthy of a standing ovation, and since there's *nothing* Leo loves more than applause, the Sake Champagne Mojito is the ideal refreshment for this celestial lion's next party.

SERVES 6

10 fresh mint leaves

1 cup granulated sugar

3 ounces lime juice

1 (25-ounce) bottle sake

1 (25-ounce) bottle champagne

6 lime slices, seeded, for garnish

In a large pitcher, use a muddler or the base of a wooden spoon to muddle mint leaves, sugar, and lime juice. Add sake and champagne. Stir mixture until sake and champagne flavors are combined. Serve in six glasses—or trendy mason jars—full of ice, garnishing each with a slice of lime.

Strawberry Daiquiri

There are many iterations of the popular Daiquiri cocktail, and while all are certainly tasty, the most Leo-esque variation is the classic Strawberry Daiquiri. During the summertime, celestial lions truly shine (after all, it is their birthday season!), and the Strawberry Daiquiri is the perfect companion for warm-weather merriment. This easy-to-make concoction blends rum, triple sec, lime juice, and strawberries, creating a deliciously boozy fruit smoothie. The Strawberry Daiquiri looks beautiful, too: when blended, the strawberries give it a gorgeous pink tint. Leos will love sipping this fabulous, tasty treat while poolside on a hot summer day.

SERVES 1

½ cup strawberries, hulled, sliced, and divided

2 ounces light rum

1 ounce lime juice

½ ounce triple sec

½ teaspoon granulated sugar

4 strawberry slices, for garnish

Chill a margarita glass in the freezer for five minutes. Combine all ingredients except garnish in a blender, and blend until smooth. Pour into chilled margarita glass, garnish with fresh strawberry slices, and get ready to party!

Tequila Mint Hot Chocolate

Even summer babies are forced to endure cold weather every now and then. Though celestial lions enjoy stretching out under the sun's warm rays, these resourceful wildcats also know how to turn up the heat on frosty nights. Leos will love to invite their closest friends and lovers over for a Tequila Mint Hot Chocolate party. This fabulous cocktail is the perfect wintry treat, seamlessly combining cocoa, tequila, chocolate chips, peppermint schnapps, and whipped cream. Yum! The soft, refreshing mint perfectly complements the tequila's distinctive flavor, creating an extremely delicious taste that is sure to leave lions purring.

SERVES 4

¼ cup cocoa powder

1 tablespoon granulated sugar

Pinch kosher salt

3 cups whole milk

4 ounces milk chocolate chips

4 ounces bittersweet chocolate chips

2 ounces peppermint schnapps

4 ounces silver tequila

Whipped cream, for garnish

4 fresh mint leaves, for garnish

In a saucepan, combine cocoa powder, sugar, and salt. Stir gently. Over medium heat, add milk, milk chocolate chips, and bittersweet chocolate chips, and continue stirring until chocolate is fully melted. Gently whisk to combine ingredients. Remove from heat and stir in peppermint schnapps and tequila. Divide hot mixture into four Irish coffee glasses. Garnish each with a dollop of whipped cream and a mint leaf.

Tequila Sunrise

Leo's astrological ruler is the sun—the powerful, radiant star that is the center of our solar system. Though these wildcats occasionally hunt at night, Leos are daylight lovers who receive their vibrant, glowing energy from the sun. Each day marks a new opportunity for Leo to shine brightly, making the Tequila Sunrise a perfect cocktail for these vivacious fire signs. The Tequila Sunrise pays homage to a breathtaking morning sky through its beautiful color gradation. Its stunning appearance is achieved by layering orange juice, grenadine, and tequila, and it is served unmixed to maintain each ingredient's dynamic hue.

SERVES 1

1½ ounces gold tequila
4 ounces orange juice
Dash grenadine
Orange slice, seeded, for garnish
Maraschino cherry, for garnish

Chill a highball glass in the freezer for five minutes. Combine tequila and orange juice in chilled highball glass. Float grenadine on top by slowly pouring it over the back of a spoon, and garnish with an orange slice and maraschino cherry. If you're planning on a long night out, a couple of these are guaranteed to keep you luminous!

Toronha

Leos love to stand out from the crowd, so the Toronha is the perfect beverage for these trendsetting lions. This delicious tequila-based concoction is relatively unknown by mainstream consumers, so Leos will pounce at the opportunity to make this beverage trendy. It's only a matter of time before the Toronha becomes ubiquitous, and Leos want to make sure they alone are responsible for starting the craze.

SERVES 1

2 ounces silver tequila
2 ounces grapefruit juice
1 tablespoon grenadine
½ ounce triple sec

Chill a margarita glass in the freezer for five minutes. Combine all ingredients in a blender filled with ice, blend until smooth, and strain into chilled margarita glass. You're a natural talent scout, darling Leo!

Whiskey Highball

High-rolling Leos will love sipping the classic Whiskey Highball. Though this traditional beverage is simply a mix of whiskey and club soda, Leos know that the highball is a class act. In fact, the Whiskey Highball's rich history dates back to the nineteenth century. Leos admire traditions of excellence, making the Whiskey Highball a delightfully desirable treat.

SERVES 1

2 ounces whiskey
4 ounces club soda

Pour whiskey over two large ice cubes in a Collins glass. Add club soda, and enjoy a timeless treat as classy as you!

White Wine Spritzer

The world is Leo's catwalk, so celestial lions are always dressed to the nines. Leos also enjoy drinks that look as good as they taste, and the White Wine Spritzer is the perfect, versatile cocktail to match Leo's many ensembles. Just as Leo's favorite little black dress can be styled up or down, the White Wine Spritzer can seamlessly transition from a day to a night cocktail. Though this refreshing cocktail has been enjoyed for generations, its recent comeback has made the White Wine Spritzer effortlessly chic. Leos will love accessorizing with this drink at their favorite rooftop parties.

SERVES 1

3 ounces chilled white wine
1 ounce chilled club soda
Lime wedge, for garnish

Pour wine into a white wine glass filled with ice. Add club soda and garnish with lime wedge for a complete presentation. The only thing that could possibly make this cocktail better is your dynamic personality, sweet Leo! Sip and enjoy!

Virgo

(AUGUST 23–SEPTEMBER 22): THE IDEALIST

Virgo is the most analytical sign of the zodiac, and Virgos value logic and thoughtful organization. Traditionally represented by the idyllic virgin, these practical earth signs are careful observers who approach life with methodological efficiency. Virgo is ruled by Mercury (the planet that governs communication), making these earthy intellectuals sharp orators and writers. Virgos are meticulous workers, and enjoy classifying, categorizing, and creating functional systems whenever possible. Perhaps most important, Virgos are phenomenal teachers and healers: they love to help others, and deeply enjoy problem-solving with a friend in need. Virgos are thoughtful and compassionate partners, and attract others through their striking intelligence and genuine compassion.

Virgos are cocktail purists. These rational thinkers favor drinks that use straightforward, practical ingredients to create classically delicious mixers. Virgos appreciate the simplicity of an elegantly stirred Vodka Martini, the refreshing herbal aromas of a Mint Julep, and the effortless effervescence of a traditional Paloma on the rocks. No need to get too fancy when preparing a cocktail for your Virgo lover or friend. These logic-based earth signs are turned off by excessive garnishes and overly complicated beverages. Virgos love measuring proportions and following recipes, making them among the best mixologists of the zodiac!

7 & 7

The 7 & 7 is truly a match made in heaven (and fittingly so, since the number seven is associated with spiritual paradise): 7UP's zesty bubbles perfectly enhance the crisp, herbal notes of Seagram's 7 Crown Blended Whiskey. Further adding to the theme of sevens, the 7 & 7 rose in popularity in the 1970s, when university students began combining their favorite soda and spirits to spark dormitory rowdiness. Despite its collegiate roots, however, Virgos of all (legal drinking) ages will love the 7 & 7's straightforward reliability. In a complicated world filled with unexplained mysteries and bizarre phenomena, the 7 & 7 is divinely dependable. And there is nothing more magic to Virgos than logic.

SERVES 1

4 ounces 7UP
1½ ounces Seagram's 7 Crown Blended Whiskey

Combine all ingredients in a highball glass filled with ice. Stir gently. Bonus points for taking your first sip *exactly* at 7:07!

Beerita

Virgos love to be helpful and to use their practical skills whenever possible. But generous Virgos must be careful: these sweet earth signs are often so accommodating that they end up becoming sponges for others people's problems. The best way to combat this, of course, is to keep things clean and uncomplicated, making the Beerita the perfect cocktail for Virgo's next party. This Margarita-inspired, beer-based beverage is delicious, fun, and extremely easy to prepare. Guests will adore this tasty refreshment, and Virgos will cherish the Beerita's hassle-free recipe. Phew, one less thing to worry about!

SERVES 6

12 ounces frozen limeade concentrate, slightly thawed and divided

2 tablespoons sea salt

24 ounces Mexican beer

1½ cups gold tequila

6 lime slices, seeded, for garnish

Prepare three bowls. In the first, add 1 tablespoon limeade. In the second, add salt. In the third, combine remaining limeade concentrate, beer, and tequila. Rim each margarita glass by dipping it first in bowl of limeade, then in bowl of salt. Divide alcohol mixture evenly among the glasses, garnishing each with a lime slice.

Boozy Iced Coffee

Virgos are diligent, hard workers who commit fully to whatever projects they begin. Though these earth signs don't like to step away from any uncompleted tasks, sometimes even the most industrious Virgos need a quick happy hour fix. On these occasions, a Boozy Iced Coffee is the perfect midday cocktail for these conscientious Virgos. This invigorating elixir kicks up the daily dose of caffeine with a healthy helping of vodka... and what could be better than instant energy with a twist? Whether burning the midnight oil or prepping for a night on the dance floor, Virgos will love sipping this stimulating refreshment.

SERVES 3

1½ cups black coffee
4 ounces whole milk
4 ounces vodka

2 tablespoons granulated sugar
2 tablespoons caramel sauce

Combine all ingredients in a pitcher, stir, and pour into hurricane glasses filled with ice. Get ready to fire up, dear Virgo!

Cable Car

Though these practical earth signs may lead with skepticism, Virgos are always intrigued by modernization. Virgos appreciate thoughtful enhancements, and will instantly fall in love with the artfully curated Cable Car. Invented in 1996 by mixologist Tony Abou-Ganim, the Cable Car was inspired by the classic Sidecar cocktail. The Cable Car combines spicy, sweet, and sour notes, forming a complex and unique flavor profile. Virgos admire skilled craftsmanship, and will appreciate the Cable Car's unusual ingredients that simultaneously contrast with and complement each other.

SERVES 1

1½ teaspoons ground cinnamon
1½ teaspoons granulated sugar
Lemon wedge
1½ ounces spiced rum

1 ounce lemon juice
1¾ ounces orange liqueur
1½ ounces simple syrup
Orange peel, for garnish

Chill a cocktail glass in the freezer for five minutes. Stir cinnamon and sugar together in a saucer. Rub the rim of chilled cocktail glass with lemon wedge, then dip the rim into cinnamon and sugar mixture to coat. Set aside. Add remaining ingredients to a shaker filled with ice. Shake vigorously, and strain into the prepared cocktail glass. Garnish with orange peel. Be careful sipping these when your ruling planet goes retrograde! Mercury governs transportation, so avoid anything—including cocktails—inspired by movement when the planet spins in reverse!

Gimlet

Virgos enjoy unpretentious, straightforward cocktails that pack a punch, making the Gimlet the ideal treat for these forthright earth signs. In the nineteenth century, British Royal Navy Rear Admiral Sir Thomas Desmond Gimlette created this concoction to protect his sailors against scurvy. Today, the Gimlet is a staple at upscale bars.

SERVES 1

2½ ounces gin
½ ounce lime juice
½ ounce simple syrup
Lime slice, seeded, for garnish

Chill a cocktail glass in the freezer for five minutes. Combine all ingredients except garnish in a shaker filled with ice. Shake well, and strain into chilled cocktail glass. Garnish with lime slice and enjoy!

Grasshopper

Virgos are the "young grasshoppers" of the zodiac: these diligent earth signs harness their inherent perfectionism to become experts, ultimately graduating from student to teacher. After a long day of apprenticeship, Virgos will love serving up these minty concoctions.

SERVES 1

3 ounces heavy cream
1 ounce crème de menthe
1 ounce white crème de cacao
Peppermint patty, for garnish

Chill a martini glass in the freezer for five minutes. Combine all ingredients except garnish in a shaker filled with ice. Shake vigorously, and serve straight up in chilled martini glass. Garnish with a peppermint patty. Though your training may have just begun...it's always happy hour somewhere.

Jack Rose

Virgos are natural analysts. These intelligent earth signs are adept at picking up on nuance, identifying hidden motives, and reading between the lines. It comes as no surprise, then, that many Virgos adore reading classic literature. Virgos love diving into compelling stories filled with dynamic characters and captivating narratives. These enchanting tales allow logical Virgos to journey into different worlds, all within the comfort (and safety) of their cozy couch. The Jack Rose is a terrific cocktail to sip while ingesting an inspiring novel: this brandy-based beverage played a prominent role in Ernest Hemingway's 1926 tale, *The Sun Also Rises*, and was also the favorite drink of author John Steinbeck. Virgos will love the Jack Rose's distinctive flavor, as well as its esteemed place in literary history.

SERVES 1

1½ ounces apple brandy
¾ ounce lemon juice

½ ounce grenadine
Lemon twist, for garnish

Combine all ingredients except garnish in a shaker filled with ice. Shake vigorously until chilled, and fine-strain into a coupe glass. Garnish with lemon twist. After a few sips, you may be inspired to write the next great novel!

Lychee Sake

If you're seeking a date-night cocktail that's both creative and uncomplicated, look no further than the Lychee Sake. This innovative beverage is both distinctive *and* straightforward, making it the ideal choice for selective Virgos. Sake (a Japanese rice wine) is an excellent cocktail base: its dry, neutral flavor seamlessly blends with the sweet, aromatic notes of the lychee fruit. Ready for the best part? Though this delicious beverage boasts an elegant presentation, it's extremely easy (and fast!) to prepare. Virgos will love this simple, fragrant elixir—that is also sure to set the mood for a romantic evening.

SERVES 2

¼ cup lychee water (from canned lychees)
½ cup sake

1 tablespoon corn syrup
6 lychees, for garnish

Pour lychee water, sake, and corn syrup into shaker filled with ice. Shake vigorously. Pour into rocks glasses and drop three lychees into each glass for garnish. These adornments also serve a practical purpose: they make deliciously boozy treats after you've finished your beverage. How delish!

Margarita

When it's time to let loose, Virgos know that the classic Margarita is the perfect cocktail to ensure a fabulous time. This popular tequila concoction is a terrific summertime companion, though its delicious, zesty flavor will be sure to heat up any season. The timeless Margarita effortlessly enhances the distinct flavor of the agave-based tequila with fresh citrus notes. Virgos will love the delectable simplicity of the Margarita's sweet and sour combination...but be careful: this potent blend is known to pack a punch. A few too many of these tasty treats, and you may suddenly end up on a hazy adventure several miles south of the border.

SERVES 1

1½ ounces silver tequila
1 ounce triple sec

¾ ounce lime juice
Lime slice, seeded, for garnish

Chill a margarita glass in the freezer for five minutes. Combine all ingredients except garnish in a shaker filled with ice. Shake, shake, shake, and strain into chilled margarita glass with fresh ice. Garnish with lime slice. *¡Delicioso!*

Mint Julep

Grab your favorite sun hat and head down to the races! Virgos will love sipping the luscious Mint Julep, the iconic bourbon-based cocktail that has been recognized as the official beverage of the Kentucky Derby since 1938. Containing only four ingredients (bourbon, mint, simple syrup, and ice), the Mint Julep is both easy to prepare and delicious, which likely explains its enduring popularity. The Mint Julep actually originated in the southern United States in the eighteenth century, making it one of the oldest cocktails still beloved today! Virgos will adore the simplicity of its fresh, classic ingredients, as well as its place as a time-honored favorite in American history.

SERVES 1

10 fresh mint leaves, divided

¼ ounce raw sugar syrup

2 ounces bourbon

Using a muddler or the back of a wooden spoon, lightly muddle nine mint leaves and raw sugar syrup in a rocks glass. Add bourbon, and pack the glass tightly with crushed ice. Stir until the cup is frosted on the outside, then top with more crushed ice to form an ice dome. Garnish with a mint leaf, and get ready to place your bet!

Mudslide

Practical Virgos adore efficiency. These logical earth signs are systems-oriented, and are naturally proficient at streamlining workflows, calendars, and activities. The Mudslide is the perfect concoction for productive Virgos, as this delicious, chocolaty beverage does double duty as both a potent cocktail and a decadent dessert. The Mudslide features three different types of liquor that produce a strong elixir, while its rich and creamy ingredients create the ideal boozy milkshake. Virgos will love this mouthwatering beverage that is guaranteed to make after-dinner indulgences a little more interesting.

SERVES 1

1 ounce vodka
1 ounce coffee liqueur
1 ounce Irish cream liqueur

1 ounce whole milk
Chocolate syrup,
    for garnish

Combine all ingredients except garnish in a blender. Blend until smooth, and pour into a hurricane glass. Drizzle with chocolate syrup to garnish. No need to judge yourself, Virgo darling—you're allowed to indulge every once in a while.

Orange Tundra

Though the Orange Tundra was only created in 2003, this colorful concoction has already made a big splash in the cocktail community. The Orange Tundra features a surprising combination of vodka, coffee liqueur, cream soda, and orange juice. When combined, this indulgent, distinctive mixture creates a frothy, creamy flavor that is both zesty and refreshing. But preparation is key: to create both the vivid golden hue and aromatic taste, the ingredients must be carefully added in precise order and left to settle without stirring. Since meticulous Virgos are great at following directions, these careful earth signs will be able to effortlessly produce the perfect Orange Tundras, making this cocktail a terrific choice for these instruction-loving earth signs.

SERVES 1

1 ounce vodka
1 ounce coffee liqueur
1 ounce cream soda

1 ounce orange juice
Maraschino cherry, for garnish

Add three ice cubes to a highball glass. Very carefully, and in the following order, pour vodka, coffee liqueur, cream soda, and orange juice into the glass. Do not stir. Garnish with a maraschino cherry and voilà: a stunning, tasty treat!

Paloma

The Paloma (Spanish for "dove") is one of the most popular cocktails in Mexico. Light and fruity, the Paloma combines tequila, grapefruit soda, and lime juice to create a sophisticated flavor profile. And it's also extremely refreshing: the Paloma's vivid citrus notes and light effervescence make it a terrific poolside companion during the hot, sultry summer days. Virgos will love cooling off with this invigorating beverage, and will also enjoy preparing this succulent cocktail. Boasting accessible ingredients and a straightforward recipe, the Paloma is guaranteed to become one of Virgo's go-to favorites.

SERVES 1

2 ounces silver tequila
½ ounce lime juice

12 ounces grapefruit soda

Add tequila and lime juice to a highball glass filled with ice. Add grapefruit soda and stir briefly. Summer has never been so refreshing!

Planter's Punch

Let's face it: most Virgos prefer a no-frills dive over a vibrant tiki bar. The highly curated island ambiance is sometimes a little too much for these straightforward earth signs, who enjoy simple ingredients, minimal embellishments, and unpretentious decor. The Planter's Punch, however, may be Virgo's gateway into a more vivacious, tropical paradise. This rum-based cocktail is one of the first island-inspired beverages, and is considered the grandfather of tiki drinks. Dating back to the late 1800s, Planter's Punch captures the essence of a timeless, seaside oasis through a simple combination of club soda, rum, pineapple juice, and grenadine. Virgos will love this pioneering, coral-colored cocktail that defines vacation.

SERVES 1

1½ ounces dark rum
2 ounces pineapple juice
¼ ounce grenadine

Club soda to fill
Seasonal fruit, for garnish

Add rum, pineapple juice, and grenadine to a shaker and shake well. Strain into a highball glass filled with ice, and top off with club soda. Garnish with seasonal fruit, lather up the sunscreen, and get ready for some fun in the sun!

Sazerac

The Sazerac may be the closest thing we have to time travel. This distinctive cocktail originated in New Orleans in the 1800s as a carefully curated blend sourced from local apothecaries. Though the ingredients have changed slightly over time, the Sazerac still carries the smoky, enchanting essence that defines the spirit of the Big Easy. Virgos will adore this steamy, alluring beverage that enhances the flavor of whiskey with a dash of absinthe—the infamous lime-green spirit associated with some of the twentieth century's most prolific artists and writers. Virgos will love the Sazerac's dynamic flavor profile, as well as its deep-rooted place in New Orleans' history.

SERVES 1

Dash absinthe

3 dashes bitters

1 sugar cube

2 ounces whiskey

Lemon peel

Chill a rocks glass in the freezer for five minutes. Pour absinthe into chilled rocks glass, and carefully swirl it around to coat the glass. Discard excess liquid and set glass aside. In a mixing glass, muddle bitters and sugar cube with a muddler or the back of a wooden spoon. Add whiskey, fill with ice, and stir. Strain mixture into prepared rocks glass. Twist a slice of lemon peel over the rim to absorb any extra oils, and discard peel.

Vodka Martini

There is perhaps no beverage as classic or elegant as the Vodka Martini. While this pioneering drink has yielded many popular spin-offs, the Vodka Martini has its own important role in cocktail history. Though the first Vodka Martini was concocted in the early 1900s, its popularity grew after World War II, when vodka became a luxury item due to the scarcity of Russian imports. In 1953, the effortlessly stylish James Bond requested his Vodka Martini "shaken, not stirred," catapulting the cocktail into the mainstream. The Vodka Martini was—and still is—the symbol of sophistication. The beverage quickly became the go-to order when impressing swanky clients over dinner, and it remains one of the most popular happy hour quenchers. Its timeless presentation and straightforward flavor make it the ideal choice for fastidious Virgos who value the understated yet iconic significance of the delectable Vodka Martini.

SERVES 1

2 ounces vodka
¾ ounce dry vermouth
Lemon twist, for garnish

Chill a cocktail glass in the freezer for five minutes and do it like Bond, Virgo darling: combine all ingredients except garnish in a cocktail shaker filled with ice, and shake vigorously. Strain into chilled cocktail glass, garnish with lemon twist, and inhale the essence of cool.

Libra

(SEPTEMBER 23–OCTOBER 22): THE CHARMER

Libras are represented by the scales, and strive for balance, harmony, and justice. This air sign maintains objectivity through its open-mindedness, making Libra the most socially fluid sign of the zodiac. Libras are charming, well liked, and effortlessly popular among their peers. These dynamic air signs can seamlessly navigate happy hours, dinner parties, and casual hangouts alike, attracting friends and lovers with their amiable, gregarious dispositions. Libra is ruled by Venus (the planet that governs romance, beauty, and money), so these stylish air signs are the aesthetic experts of the zodiac. Dapper Libras enjoy connoisseurship, and can be found sipping wine in a vineyard, applauding modern artwork at a gallery, or shopping for the latest designer threads. Libras enjoy the company of others, and appreciate spending time with their friends, family, and partners.

Libras are renowned for their highbrow taste, and favor cocktails that reflect their sophisticated constitutions. Presentation is everything for these debonair air signs: Libras admire elegant stemware, tasteful garnishes, and meticulously measured proportions (after all, their sign is symbolized by the scales). Cocktails are luxury items for Libras, so drinks like the graceful French 75, iconic Metropolitan, and enthralling Bourbon Chai Toddy will perfectly complement Libra's flawless finesse. Libras despise imbalance, so these air signs should avoid drinks that are disproportioned. Though it takes practice to become an expert bartender, just be sure that whatever drinks you mix up for Libra are delicious, smooth, and harmonious.

Appletini

Suave Libras can seamlessly navigate any social situation, fluidly gliding between soirées, gallery openings, happy hours, and book clubs. These charming, affable air signs love to accessorize with stylish cocktails that capture their socialite sensibilities. The Appletini is the perfect complement for Libras seeking delicious arm candy for a glamorous night on the town. This vibrant green beverage found stardom in the mid-1990s when it was popularized by the Los Angeles elite, and became Hollywood's go-to cocktail. To this day, the fun and flavorful Appletini is associated with the beau monde, making it an obvious choice for in-vogue Libras.

SERVES 1

1½ ounces vodka
1 ounce green apple schnapps

¼ ounce lemon juice
Apple slice, for garnish

Chill a cocktail glass in the freezer for five minutes. Combine all ingredients except garnish in a shaker filled with ice. Shake well, and strain into chilled cocktail glass. Add apple slice for garnish, touch up your lipstick, and get ready for a fabulous evening!

Basilico

Though the Basilico is a relatively new drink (it was created in 2004), it has already earned a stellar reputation within the cocktail community. The distinctive ingredient in this vodka-based beverage is basil, which is enhanced through lemon liqueur and lemon juice. Both sweet and savory, the textural Basilico features a peppery essence with an aftertaste of mint and citrus. But the key to unlocking this drink's unique fragrance is all in the wrist. To release the Basilico's full aromatic potential, the basil must be muddled to perfection. This well-balanced drink is a terrific fit for Libras, who will appreciate the complementary flavors, as well as the opportunity to sharpen their bartending skills.

SERVES 1

7 fresh basil leaves, divided
2 ounces vodka
½ ounce lemon liqueur
½ ounce lemon juice
½ ounce simple syrup

Using a muddler or the base of a wooden spoon, muddle six basil leaves in the base of a mixing shaker. Add remaining ingredients, fill shaker with ice, and shake vigorously. Strain into an old-fashioned glass filled with crushed ice, and garnish with a basil leaf.

Bourbon Chai Toddy

Libras are ruled by Venus—the celestial body that governs beauty, romance, and earthly delights. The fragrant fusion of herbs and spices in the Bourbon Chai Toddy will be sure to satiate Libra's Venusian sensibilities by offering a fully immersive, sensory experience.

SERVES 1

1 ounce chai tea
1 tablespoon honey
1 ounce bourbon
½ ounce orange liqueur
Splash bitters
Cinnamon stick, for garnish

Prepare hot chai tea and pour into an Irish coffee glass. Add remaining ingredients except garnish, and stir well. Garnish with cinnamon stick. Sip slowly (contents are hot!) and enjoy this delicious, liquid embrace. So cozy!

Derby

For generations, southern aristocracy gathered for the iconic Kentucky Derby. Libras are always enchanted by the elite, but for those air signs who haven't attended such formal affairs, the Derby cocktail is the perfect alternative. Oh-so-sophisticated, this concoction will transform any happy hour into a high-society soirée.

SERVES 1

1 ounce bourbon whiskey
¾ ounce lime juice
½ ounce sweet vermouth
½ ounce orange liqueur
Lime wedge, for garnish

Chill a cocktail glass in the freezer for five minutes. Combine all ingredients except garnish in a cocktail shaker filled with ice. Shake well, and strain into chilled cocktail glass. Garnish with lime wedge and don't forget to curtsy!

Fog Cutter

In the 1950s, the tiki bar movement swept the nation. As World War II soldiers returned home from their stations in the South Pacific, they brought with them an appetite for island culture. The two bars pioneering this movement were Don the Beachcomber and Trader Vic's. Both located in California, these watering holes were fueled by a healthy competition that revolutionized mixology. Each new drink sparked a battle and, in the case of the Fog Cutter, the winner was clear. Though this potent libation was invented by Tony Ramos at Don the Beachcomber, it was quickly (and successfully) repackaged by Trader Vic's, and has since become synonymous with the popular tiki chain. Libras will love the captivating history of this classic cocktail, as well as the carefully chosen ingredients that guarantee a serious kick.

SERVES 1

2 ounces orange juice
1½ ounces white rum
1 ounce lemon juice
½ ounce orgeat liqueur

½ ounce gin
½ ounce brandy
½ ounce sherry
Fresh mint leaf, for garnish

Combine all ingredients except sherry and garnish in a cocktail shaker filled with ice. Shake vigorously and strain into a highball glass filled with ice. Carefully pour sherry over the drink, and garnish with mint. Go easy, sailor: this drink is notoriously powerful. According to Trader Vic, the name is a misnomer—"after two of these, you won't even see the stuff."

French 75

Symbolized by the scales, Libras aspire to create equilibrium in all areas of life. The French 75 exquisitely balances both beauty and substance, making it the ideal cocktail for symmetry-focused Libras. On the outside, the French 75 is elegant and alluring: this champagne-based beverage is recognized for its exquisite, sparkling appearance. The drink itself, however, is not for the faint of heart: this potent concoction packs a serious punch. In fact, one sip feels like being shelled in the gut by a French 75 mm cannon—a comparison that inspired its iconic name. Libras will adore this poised elixir that perfectly epitomizes harmony.

SERVES 1

1 ounce gin
½ ounce lemon juice
½ ounce simple syrup
3 ounces champagne
Lemon twist, for garnish

Combine all ingredients except champagne and garnish in a shaker filled with ice. Shake well and strain into a flute glass. Add champagne, and garnish with lemon twist. Voilà!

Frozen Margarita

The Frozen Margarita is the perfect boozy, summertime slushy. This terrifically tart, icy mix combines tequila, lime juice, and orange liqueur to create a cooling citrus concoction that is the ideal refreshment for a sweltering day. While cocktail purists may balk at the Margarita's frozen variation, stylish Libras adore this frosty treat. Libra is the most aesthetic sign of the zodiac, and these presentation-conscious air signs will appreciate the Frozen Margarita's distinctive, lavish look. Blended to perfection, the Frozen Margarita also boasts an impeccably balanced flavor profile, which will make it an instant favorite with Libras—who are inherently captivated by beauty.

SERVES 1

½ lime

Sea salt

2 ounces silver tequila

1 ounce fresh lime juice

¾ ounce orange liqueur

Lime slice, seeded, for garnish

Rub lime across rim of a margarita glass and dip glass into a saucer of sea salt. Put aside, and combine all ingredients except garnish in a blender filled with ice. Blend until mixture is smooth and frothy, then pour into the salted margarita glass. Garnish with fresh lime slice. But be careful, Libra: this drink is so delicious, you may be tempted to gulp it down. Sip slowly to avoid an annoying brain freeze!

Gin and Juice

Libras have excellent taste. These sophisticated air signs are known for their highbrow interests, discerning aesthetics, and cultured palates. So when Snoop Dogg (a proud Libra) rapped about the distinctive combination of gin and juice in his 1993 hit single, trust that he was making an *excellent* recommendation. The Gin and Juice cocktail is a deliciously fruity refreshment that effortlessly blends gin's aromatic, herbal notes with the zesty tang of grapefruit juice. Libras will love crafting this classic concoction that not only tastes great, but comes with its own theme song.

SERVES 1

1½ ounces gin
Grapefruit juice to fill

Fill a Collins glass with ice and pour in gin. Fill with juice and stir. Lay back, sip, and make sure to keep your mind on your money (and vice versa).

Hot Gin Punch

Libra is represented by the air element. Air is a conduit: it breathes life into the three other astrological elements (fire, earth, and water) by enhancing their personal dispositions. Accordingly, Libras are highly socially adept. These fun-loving air signs enjoy entertaining their friends and family by hosting spirited events throughout the year. Libras will delight in preparing and serving Hot Gin Punch for their next wintertime gathering. This aromatic recipe combines two types of booze (gin and sherry) with sugar, spice, and everything nice (in this case, fruits and honey) to create an irresistibly fragrant warmth that Libra's guests will simply adore...and nothing makes Libra happier than an epic party.

SERVES 20

24 ounces gin
24 ounces sherry
3 ounces honey
1 ounce lemon juice
1 teaspoon ground cinnamon
1 teaspoon brown sugar
Pinch ground nutmeg

6 lemon twists, for garnish
3 large pineapple chunks,
 for garnish
20 orange slices, seeded,
 for garnish
Whole cloves, for garnish

Combine all ingredients except garnishes in a large saucepan and let simmer over low heat for twenty minutes. Strain and pour hot mixture into a punch bowl with pineapple chunks and lemon twists for garnish. Serve in Irish coffee glasses. For an extra memorable presentation (an essential for aesthetic Libras), garnish each glass with an orange slice studded with cloves.

Le Fleur de Paradis

Venusian Libras adore cocktails that offer a completely enveloping experience, making Le Fleur de Paradis the perfect libation for sensory Libras. Combining a carefully curated assortment of tastes, textures, and aromas, Le Fleur de Paradis is a deliciously robust and elegant refreshment. The verdant flavors of gin and elderflower liqueur pair perfectly with the zest of lemon and grapefruit juices, while the champagne provides a sparkling touch that defines this cocktail's spirit. It's attractive, delectable, and extremely potent; Libras will fall in love with this heavenly concoction that lives up to its name.

SERVES 1

2 ounces gin
¾ ounce elderflower liqueur
½ ounce lemon juice
½ ounce grapefruit juice
¼ ounce simple syrup
Dash orange bitters
1 ounce champagne
Pansy flower, for garnish

Combine all ingredients except champagne and garnish in a shaker filled with ice. Shake vigorously, and strain into a cocktail glass. Add champagne and garnish with an edible pansy flower for a ravishing presentation. *Très magnifique!*

Lycheetini

The lychee fruit—originally from China—is luscious and sweet, with a tangy aftertaste reminiscent of green grapes. The dynamic savor of the lychee fruit makes for a terrific cocktail base, and elegant Libras will love this superb beverage. Offering a new twist on the classic martini, the Lycheetini combines vodka and lychee liqueur with a dash of lime juice to create a zesty, yet subtle, concoction. Libras will also enjoy preparing this poised cocktail: though the ingredients may be considered specialty items (depending on your region and grocery store offerings), the recipe is extremely straightforward. As easy to mix as it is to sip, the Lycheetini is an excellent choice for urbane Libras.

SERVES 1

1½ ounces vodka
1½ ounces lychee liqueur

Dash lime juice
Lychee, for garnish

Chill a cocktail glass in the freezer for five minutes. Combine all ingredients except garnish in a cocktail shaker filled with ice. Shake well, and strain into chilled cocktail glass. For extra flair (and a delicious post-beverage treat), drop lychee garnish into the cocktail before serving.

Metropolitan

Cultured Libras will love the Metropolitan cocktail. Though this brandy-based concoction originated in the 1930s, it faded into obscurity for the majority of the twentieth century. In fact, it wasn't until the cocktail craze of the 1990s that the Metropolitan was resurrected (interestingly, its close cousin—the Cosmopolitan—was also rediscovered at this time, though the Cosmopolitan ultimately exploded in popularity after becoming the unofficial signature drink of *Sex and the City*). Stylish Libras will adore this delicious, in-the-know beverage that exudes modern sophistication while also capturing the timeless essence of chic, urban life.

SERVES 1

2 ounces brandy

1 ounce sweet vermouth

½ teaspoon simple syrup

2 dashes bitters

Chill a cocktail glass in the freezer for five minutes. Combine all ingredients in a cocktail shaker filled with ice. Shake well, and strain into chilled cocktail glass. Stylish and sophisticated—yes, this beverage is absolutely *perfect* for you, darling Libra!

Mimosa

There is no meal that suits Libras' lighthearted temperament better than brunch. This cheerful and leisurely weekend feast provides a terrific excuse to get dressed up (and show off your favorite new outfit, of course), link up with friends, and indulge in delectable foods and midday booze. And when it comes to daytime drinking, there is no smarter choice than the Mimosa. Mimosas are brunch essentials, and with good reason: the bright, vivid flavors of orange juice are seamlessly enriched by the champagne's buoyancy, creating a super drinkable, lively concoction. This light, bubbly cocktail is fun and extremely simple to prepare, making it the perfect accessory for afternoon indulgence.

SERVES 1

2 ounces orange juice   Champagne to fill

Add orange juice to a champagne flute, and top off with champagne. Pour champagne gently to avoid spillover (though, after a few of these, over-pouring may be inevitable).

Negroni

Libras will love sipping the sophisticated Negroni cocktail. Though its exact origins are unknown, this beverage was first developed in Italy over one hundred years ago. The Negroni's defining ingredient is Campari—an Italian bitter liqueur with a vivid crimson hue (originally derived from crushed cochineal insects). Libras will delight in this worldly cocktail with a distinguished flavor: the Campari's sharp notes are counterbalanced by the sweet vermouth and aromatic gin. With equal parts of each ingredient, this drink is also extremely easy to prepare, making it the choice cocktail to serve friends or lovers who share Libra's passion for la dolce vita.

SERVES 1

1 ounce Campari

1 ounce gin

1 ounce sweet vermouth

½ orange slice, seeded, for garnish

Combine all ingredients except garnish in an old-fashioned glass filled with ice. Stir mixture until glass is cold. Garnish with orange slice. Now *that's amore!*

Rum and Coke

Represented by the scales, Libra symbolizes partnership. These air signs value sets of two, and believe that the greatest whole is achieved by two equally weighted parts. When it comes to dynamic duos, there are few ingredients more perfectly paired than rum and Coke. The spicy vibrancy of rum is effortlessly enhanced by cola's sweet carbonation, and the combined flavors yield a distinctive, highly satisfying drink that's well suited for any occasion. Libras will adore this easy-to-prepare, classic combination that epitomizes the spirit of a happy couple.

SERVES 1

2 ounces dark rum
6 ounces cola
Lime wedge, for garnish

Pour rum into a highball glass filled with ice and add cola. Garnish with a lime wedge. Cheers!

Tuxedo

While many signs dread events that require formal wear, Libras eagerly await the occasion. Dapper Libras always enjoy looking their best; in fact, some Libras actually *prefer* black tie to casual wear. Ruled by Venus, Libras enjoy any demonstrations of luxury, making the Tuxedo cocktail a terrific choice for these posh air signs. Interestingly, the Tuxedo beverage and famous suit were invented in tandem: in the late 1800s, New York's social elite were defining their unique style in Tuxedo Park—a Hudson Valley enclave for high society—and both the cocktail and ensemble were named after this swanky region. Although the formal suit became more widely known than the beverage, the Tuxedo cocktail is still the perfect accessory for any dignified affair.

SERVES 1

1½ ounces gin
1½ ounces dry vermouth
¼ teaspoon maraschino liqueur

¼ teaspoon anise liqueur
2 dashes bitters
Maraschino cherry, for garnish

Chill a cocktail glass in the freezer for five minutes. Combine all ingredients except garnish in a mixing glass filled with ice. Stir and strain mixture into chilled cocktail glass. Garnish with maraschino cherry and be prepared to turn heads with this perfectly swanky liquid accessory.

Scorpio

(OCTOBER 23–NOVEMBER 21): THE ENCHANTER

Scorpios have a bit of a reputation. These mysterious water signs are renowned for their spellbinding allure and relentless ambition, making them the most enigmatic signs of the zodiac. Scorpios are represented by the scorpion—the infamous arachnid that dwells in the shadows, only revealing itself when prompted to attack. Life is a chess game for Scorpios, whose deliberate maneuvers always ensure the ultimate "checkmate." Scorpio is ruled by Pluto—the celestial body (named after the mythological god of the underworld) that governs death, sex, and transformation. Evolution is paramount for Scorpios, who use regeneration as a tool to prompt emotional growth and psychic expansion. Scorpios entice friends and lovers with their bewitching magnetism. Scorpios are brave, ambitious, and passionate partners, who value loyalty and intimacy in all relationships.

Scorpios are powerful creatures who demand equally potent cocktails. These enchanting water signs aren't afraid to get intense by pushing boundaries with their favorite edgy libations. Scorpios will love brooding over a Dark 'n' Stormy, exploring their macabre side with Death in the Afternoon, or highlighting their signature feature with the Stinger.

When preparing a drink for a Scorpio, avoid dainty libations that are excessively flowery or sweet. These dynamic water signs are uninspired by anything overtly polite or innocent. Scorpios know that the best cocktails are hypnotic, complex, and sensual...a perfect match for this sign's most distinctive attributes!

Beer Punch

When Scorpios entertain, there is always an element of surprise. Scorpios love shock value, so their preferred party cocktails will always feature an unanticipated kick. Beer Punch is a fabulous choice for Scorpio's next summertime hang. This delicious beverage combines fresh fruit—strawberries and blueberries—with grenadine and lime juice to create a tropical, citrusy tang. Unlike traditional punches, however, this recipe's sole alcohol is light beer, which produces a bright and buoyant base. Scorpios will love sharing this delightful and unexpected warm-weather refreshment with guests.

SERVES 4

4 strawberries, hulled and sliced
¼ cup blueberries
¼ cup granulated sugar
2 tablespoons grenadine
2 tablespoons lime juice
2 (12-ounce) bottles light beer

Add strawberries, blueberries, sugar, grenadine, and lime juice to a mixing glass. Use a muddler or the base of a wooden spoon to muddle until sugar is dissolved, then cover with plastic wrap and refrigerate for one hour, stirring periodically to draw out berry juices. To serve, pour mixture into four rocks glasses. Pour six ounces of beer into each glass and stir gently.

Black Russian

Ahh, the legendary Black Russian. Invented in 1949, the Black Russian is a strong and straightforward concoction that contains two parts vodka and one part coffee liqueur. Both extremely easy to prepare and superbly delicious, the Black Russian reigned supreme across the United States for almost two decades. In fact, it sparked the popular, creamy vari-ant (appropriately titled the White Russian) that emerged in the 1960s. Though the White Russian is certainly tasty, Scorpios will prefer sipping the original blend that boasts undiluted potency. Chic and punchy, the Black Russian is sure to become one of Scorpio's favorite cocktails.

SERVES 1

2 ounces vodka
1 ounce coffee liqueur

Combine all ingredients in a mixing glass filled with ice. Stir, and strain into an old-fashioned glass over fresh ice.

Black Widow

Did you know that spiders and scorpions are distant cousins? Thanks to their eight legs, both creatures are classified as arachnids. And what better way to pay homage to Scorpio's genus than the Black Widow cocktail? Scorpios will love sipping this tequila-based cocktail named after their infamous relatives. This delicious refreshment combines fresh blackberries and basil leaves, creating a tart and herbal concoction. Boasting a hypnotizing crimson hue (achieved through the muddled blackberries), the Black Widow cocktail creates a wonderfully spooky ambiance. The Black Widow is an excellent beverage to serve around Halloween...which just so happens to correspond with Scorpio's birthday season!

SERVES 1

3 blackberries, divided
3 fresh basil leaves, divided
1½ ounces silver tequila
1 ounce lime juice
1 teaspoon agave nectar

Using a muddler or the base of a wooden spoon, muddle two blackberries and two basil leaves in a shaker. Add remaining ingredients and fill shaker with ice. Shake well. Strain into a martini glass filled with fresh ice. Skewer a blackberry and basil leaf onto a toothpick to garnish.

Bloody Mary

Macabre Scorpios may be familiar with the Bloody Mary ritual: to conjure Bloody Mary's tormented soul, stand in a dark or candlelit room and chant her name three times into a mirror. This ghastly folktale began in the early twentieth century, around the same time the cocktail was invented. Though there is no *proven* link between the phantom and the beverage, Scorpios will be sure to appreciate this blood-red drink that inadvertently alludes to the ultra-eerie legend. Who knows: after a few of these, Scorpios may be inclined to summon their own ghosts...by texting an ex or two.

SERVES 1

3 ounces tomato juice
1½ ounces vodka
½ ounce lemon juice
Dash Worcestershire sauce

Pinch celery salt
Pinch ground black pepper
Celery stalk, for garnish

Combine all ingredients except garnish in a highball glass over ice. Stir well and garnish with celery stalk. With flavors this delicious, it's easy to believe in the supernatural!

Bourbon Cherry Coke

Water signs derive power through their emotional depth, causing Scorpios to be extremely sentimental. Accordingly, Scorpios adore anything vintage: this water sign loves feeling connected to the past, and enjoys reflecting on the sights, sounds, and styles of bygone times. Scorpios are particularly drawn to mid-century aesthetics, including 1950s elements. The Bourbon Cherry Coke is the perfect cocktail for Scorpios who want to evoke the spirit of a retro soda shop. This clever beverage blends fresh cherries (muddled to enhance their natural flavor) with bourbon and cola, creating a sweet, bubbly concoction with a serious kick.

SERVES 2

1¼ cups fresh cherries, pitted
1 teaspoon granulated sugar
4 ounces bourbon whiskey
12 ounces cola

Using a muddler or the base of a wooden spoon, muddle cherries, sugar, and bourbon in a mixing glass. Split mixture between two highball glasses filled with ice, and add cola. Serve with a straw. Don't forget, dear Scorpio: while the flavors may be reminiscent of your younger days, this beverage is *far* from innocent.

Corpse Reviver

Scorpios will love this timeless "hair of the dog" cocktail. Though early iterations of the uplifting Corpse Reviver date back to the mid-1800s, the recipe that is still enjoyed today was first printed in 1930. The cocktail was prescribed "to be taken before 11 a.m., or whenever steam and energy are needed." This dynamic elixir combines cognac, apple brandy, and sweet vermouth to induce a drastic jolt to the system, guaranteed to "revive" the weary and hungover. Ghoulish Scorpios will delight in this pungent concoction that is sure to wake the dead.

SERVES 1

1½ ounces cognac
¾ ounce apple brandy

¾ ounce sweet vermouth

Chill a cocktail glass in the freezer for five minutes. Combine all ingredients in a cocktail shaker filled with ice and stir well. Strain into chilled cocktail glass. After a few sips of this, you'll be ready to rise from the ashes.

Dark 'n' Stormy

Scorpios are enchanted by the mysterious and supernatural. These spooky water signs love ghost stories, and every Scorpio knows that some of the most eerie tales begin with the classic opening: "'Twas a dark and stormy night." Scorpios will delight sipping on the drink that captures this haunted spirit: the Dark 'n' Stormy. The Dark 'n' Stormy is a rum and ginger beer cocktail that was invented by Caribbean sailors. Legend has it that the name was derived from the drink's murky, amber hue that was described as "the color of a cloud only a fool or dead man would sail under." Between the cocktail's enchanting lure and mouthwatering sweet-and-spicy flavors, the Dark 'n' Stormy is sure to become one of Scorpio's go-to refreshments.

SERVES 1

1½ ounces dark rum
12 ounces ginger beer

Lime wedge, for garnish

Fill a highball glass with ice and pour in rum, followed by ginger beer. Garnish with lime wedge and enjoy this spellbinding libation!

Death in the Afternoon

Literary Scorpios will adore Death in the Afternoon, which was invented by author (and serious drinker) Ernest Hemingway. The cocktail shares its name with Hemingway's 1932 classic book on bullfighting, though its recipe was first printed in a 1935 collection of celebrity recipes. His instructions: "Pour one jigger absinthe into a Champagne glass. Add iced Champagne until it attains the proper opalescent milkiness. Drink three to five of these slowly." While it may not be the *best* idea to follow Hemingway's serving recommendations, Scorpios will love this decadent, potent beverage that blends absinthe and champagne to create an herbal, silky flavor.

SERVES 1

1½ ounces absinthe
4½ ounces champagne

Though Hemingway offered more romantic directions, simply create your drink by pouring absinthe into a champagne flute and adding champagne.

Envy Cocktail

Scorpios are ruled by Pluto—the celestial body that governs death, sex, rebirth, and transformation. On a good day, Plutonian energy can inspire growth through emotional healing and spiritual regeneration. When provoked, however, Pluto's power-hungry influence can incite resentment and jealousy. When these spiteful feelings start to boil over, Scorpios will love stirring up the Envy Cocktail. This turquoise-toned, tequila-based beverage is delicious, refreshing, and extremely alluring. Strikingly vibrant, this fruity drink will be sure to turn heads. Scorpios will enjoy quelling their own green-eyed monster by mixing an elixir guaranteed to become the object of *everyone else's* desire.

SERVES 1

1½ ounces silver tequila
½ ounce blue curaçao
¼ ounce pineapple juice
Maraschino cherry, for garnish

Chill a cocktail glass in the freezer for five minutes. Combine all ingredients except garnish in a cocktail shaker filled with ice. Shake well. Strain into chilled cocktail glass and garnish with maraschino cherry. But be warned, Scorpio: this eye-catching beverage has been known to provoke strong desire. Proceed with caution.

Mulled Wine

Scorpios are quite mysterious. These elusive water signs dwell in the shadows, revealing their power in furtive and unexpected ways, acting only after much deliberation and observation. Mulled Wine is the perfect cocktail for stealthy Scorpios. This traditional elixir adds seductive spices, herbs, and citrus notes to red wine, creating an aromatic blend that builds heat from the inside. Served warm, Mulled Wine is the ideal beverage to sip during the cold winter months. But don't be fooled by its charming fragrance: Mulled Wine is spiked with brandy, and much like Scorpios, the potency of this toasty libation may take you by surprise.

SERVES 4

1 (25-ounce) bottle sweet
  red wine
1 orange, peeled, sliced,
  and seeded
Orange peel
10 whole cloves
3 cinnamon sticks
¼ cup brandy
⅓ cup honey
1 teaspoon ground ginger

Combine all ingredients in a large pot over low heat for twenty-five minutes. Stir occasionally to completely dissolve honey. Ladle mixture into Irish coffee glasses to serve up a fabulous affair!

Red Sangria

Sangria is a refreshing, wine-based cocktail that is a quick, easy, and delicious party staple. Though its exact origins remain unknown, the drink is believed to have been invented in the Iberian Peninsula in the 1700s. Derived from the Spanish word for "blood" (*sangre*), historians posit that Sangria was initially created to put practical use to inferior batches of wine—fruits and brandy would mask any sour tastes. The United States was first introduced to Sangria during the 1964 World's Fair, and it quickly became a household name. Scorpios will love this dynamic, blood-red beverage that serves up both a striking presentation and a delicious, sparkling flavor.

SERVES 6

1 (25-ounce) bottle sweet
   red wine
1 lemon, wedged
1 orange, wedged

1½ ounces brandy
2 tablespoons granulated
   sugar
2 cups club soda

Pour wine into a pitcher and squeeze in juice from lemon and orange wedges. When finished, add in leftover pulp and rind. Add brandy and sugar, and chill overnight to enhance flavors. Before serving, add club soda for a bubbly sensation.

Rusty Nail

You definitely don't want to step on a rusty nail...but you may want to sip one. Not an *actual* rusty nail, of course, but the whiskey-based cocktail. This simple and sophisticated beverage originated in the 1930s, but took a few decades to find its footing. It wasn't until the 1960s that the Rat Pack discovered and became enamored by the Rusty Nail, propelling this alluring blend into mainstream mixology. After its unofficial endorsement by the crew of famous crooners, the Rusty Nail became associated with old-school glamour and panache. Scorpios will love this slow-sipping, classic beverage that defines highbrow elegance.

SERVES 1

1½ ounces whiskey
¾ ounce Drambuie

Combine all ingredients in an old-fashioned glass filled with ice, and stir well. After a few sips, you'll be sure you hit the nail on the head!

Salty Dog

Scorpios will love cooling off with the Salty Dog. This delicious beverage combines gin and grapefruit juice—each ingredient complementing the herbal and citrus flavors of the other—to create an effortlessly blended aromatic tang. But the defining feature of this cocktail is, fittingly, the glass's salted rim. Named after the slang expression for a sailor who's spent the majority of his life aboard a ship, the Salty Dog's briny accent captures the nautical essence of this timeless treat. Watery Scorpios will enjoy serving up this spirited cocktail during humid, balmy summer days.

SERVES 1

4 teaspoons sea salt
1½ ounces gin
3 ounces grapefruit juice
Grapefruit slice, seeded, for garnish

Rim a highball glass with salt and set aside. In a shaker, add gin and grapefruit juice, shaking vigorously. Pour over ice in prepared highball glass and garnish with a grapefruit slice. *Ahoy, matey!*

Scorpion

Behold, Scorpio's signature drink—literally! Much like this transformative water sign, the Scorpion is a tiki cocktail that has continued to evolve over the years. Legend has it that Trader Vic—the American entrepreneur who helped popularize tiki culture in the continental United States—modeled the Scorpion cocktail after a traditional Hawaiian punch that contained okolehao (an extremely concentrated, indigenous spirit referred to as "Hawaiian moonshine"). Though Trader Vic replaced okolehao with rum (the staple of all American tiki drinks), he recreated the elixir's defining sting by combining brandy, citrus juices, and orgeat liqueur. Scorpios will love their cocktail namesake that perfectly mirrors the sign's distinctive power.

SERVES 1

2 ounces light rum

2 ounces orange juice

¾ ounce lemon juice

½ ounce brandy

½ ounce orgeat liqueur

Orange slice, seeded, for garnish

Combine all ingredients except garnish in a cocktail shaker half-filled with ice. Shake until cold (approximately twenty seconds). Strain into a Collins glass filled with ice. Garnish with orange slice, serve with a long straw, and get ready for the cocktail's mighty prick!

Snakebite

Scorpios may be surprised to discover that the scorpion isn't the only symbol associated with their astrological sign. In addition to their namesake celestial creature, Scorpios are also associated with the eagle (which represents spiritual enlightenment) and the snake (which represents sexuality and temptation). Scorpios will love the Snakebite cocktail, which captures the dangerous allure of the slithering serpent. This potent brew combines equal parts hard cider and lager, creating an extremely intoxicating elixir. In fact, the Snakebite is so powerful that it is illegal to serve the beverage in the United Kingdom. Scorpios won't be afraid to face this edgy cocktail—but remember to take it slow to avoid venom overload.

SERVES 1

8 ounces chilled hard cider
8 ounces chilled lager

Chill a pint glass in the freezer for five minutes. Slowly combine all ingredients in chilled pint glass. Go easy, and good luck.

Stinger

Celestial scorpions are among the most enigmatic signs of the zodiac. Unlike the other fierce astrological animals (the ram, the bull, and the lion), scorpions aren't boldly assertive. These arachnids move in darkness, squeezing into crevices and lurking in corners. Though scorpions leave a small footprint, they possess one of the most powerful weapons: a venomous stinger. Scorpios will adore the powerful libation that is reminiscent of this mighty feature. Both easy to prepare and to sip, the Stinger cocktail blends two parts cognac with one part crème de menthe, creating a sweet, minty elixir that is the perfect after-dinner drink.

SERVES 1

2 ounces cognac
1 ounce white crème de menthe

Combine all ingredients in a shaker filled with ice. Shake, and strain into an old-fashioned glass filled with crushed ice. Be careful: this cocktail is incredibly sippable, and just as a Scorpio's sting is painless at first, it may appear benign. But don't be fooled—this beverage packs a serious punch!

Sagittarius

(NOVEMBER 22–DECEMBER 21): THE EXPLORER

Sagittarius, the last fire sign of the zodiac, is represented by the archer. Those born under the Sagittarius constellation embody the archer's adventurous spirit by traveling incredible distances to satisfy their curiosities. Sagittarians are natural philosophers, and these exuberant thrill-seekers are recognized for their insatiable wanderlust, captivating storytelling, and worldly sensibilities. Sagittarius is ruled by Jupiter (the planet that governs luck and expansion), so fortune follows these intrepid fire signs. Freedom is of the utmost importance for Sagittarians, who will stop at nothing to feed their desire for knowledge. Quick-witted Sagittarians are engaging and dynamic, easily recognized for their clever humor and infectious laughter. These archers are the life of every party, and attract friends and lovers through their effortless magnetism and straightforward communication style. Whether standing in line at the airport, enrolling in (yet another) academic program, or belting into a microphone at karaoke night, Sagittarians always lead with courage and enthusiasm.

Sagittarians believe that everything—including cocktails—should be an adventure. These fire signs love drinks that feature the flavors of faraway lands, so don't be surprised if you find a Sagittarius floating down a Tahitian river with a Mai Tai, dancing at the Carnival of Brazil with a Caipirinha, or exploring the Central American coast with a Panama cocktail in hand. So don't bother presenting Sagittarius with a simple mixed drink: if these fire signs aren't excited, they'll be sure to find stimulation elsewhere.

Aviation

Sagittarians will adore the Aviation cocktail, a vibrant beverage that captures the spirit of innovation and fortitude. Created in New York in the early twentieth century, the Aviation's popularity soared...until Prohibition took effect in 1920. Many early cocktails were impervious to the dry era, as illegal liquor was available through the black market. The Aviation, however, had one key issue: its primary ingredient—the purple-hued crème de violette that is derived from violet flowers—was so specialized that it disappeared completely. In fact, it wasn't until 2007 (almost one hundred years later!) that the United States resumed importing this fragrant liqueur. With its defining component finally available again, Sagittarians will love sipping on this delicious cocktail with an equally tantalizing history.

SERVES 1

2 ounces gin
¾ ounce lemon juice
½ ounce maraschino liqueur

¼ ounce crème de violette
Maraschino cherry, for garnish

Combine all ingredients except garnish in a shaker filled with ice. Shake, and strain into a cocktail glass. Garnish with maraschino cherry and up you go!

Bahama Mama

Fiery Sagittarians are the life of every party. Known for their incredible intellect, humor, and sharp tongues, Sagittarians always make a lasting impression. The Bahama Mama is the perfect companion for vivacious archers: this playful tiki classic combines four types of spirits (high-proof rum, dark rum, coconut liqueur, and coffee liqueur) with pineapple and lemon juice to a create a punchy, island-inspired flavor profile. Perfectly mirroring Sagittarians' natural ability to use comedy to mask biting remarks (hey, don't worry—we totally get it), the Bahama Mama's vivid citrus flavors mask the cocktail's extreme potency. Sagittarians will love this beachy favorite that is guaranteed to spice up any event.

SERVES 1

4 ounces pineapple juice
½ ounce lemon juice
½ ounce dark rum
½ ounce coconut liqueur

¼ ounce coffee liqueur
¼ ounce 151-proof rum
Fresh strawberry, for garnish

Combine all ingredients except garnish in a cocktail shaker filled with ice. Shake well, and strain into a hurricane glass filled with ice. Garnish with fresh strawberry, sip slowly, and enjoy!

Blue Lagoon

It's not easy to pull off neon-colored cocktails, but Sagittarians have a certain je ne sais quoi: not only can these fiery archers get away with ordering vibrant, azure-hued beverages, but they actually look good doing it! The Blue Lagoon is the quintessential aquamarine refreshment. This vodka-based cocktail grew in popularity during the 1970s, when it became the go-to drink for groovy, tropical-themed hangs. The electric Blue Lagoon is easy to prepare, consisting only of vodka, blue curaçao, and lemonade. Sagittarians will love this deliciously tangy throwback that always knows how to make a statement.

SERVES 1

1 ounce vodka
1 ounce blue curaçao

Lemonade, to fill
Maraschino cherry, for garnish

Pour vodka and curaçao into hurricane glass filled with ice. Top off with lemonade, and garnish with a maraschino cherry. Don't be surprised when you turn some heads: these cocktails are anything but shy!

Caesar

Veni, vedi, vici. The appropriately titled Caesar cocktail has built a small empire. Invented in 1969, this Alberta-born beverage became an overnight sensation. Today, the Caesar is recognized as the national drink of Canada, and with good reason: Canadians drink over 350 million servings annually. The Clamato juice creates a briny essence that is further enhanced through Worcestershire sauce, hot sauce, and pepper. Rich, delicious, and distinctive, the Caesar may ultimately topple the Bloody Mary's American reign.

SERVES 1

Lime wedge
Celery salt
Kosher salt
4 ounces Clamato juice
1½ ounces vodka

2 dashes Worcestershire
    sauce
Dash hot sauce
Pinch ground black pepper
Celery stick, for garnish

Rub the rim of a highball glass with lime wedge, and dip into saucer of celery salt and regular salt mix. Fill glass with ice and add Clamato juice, vodka, Worcestershire sauce, hot sauce, and pepper. Stir well, and garnish with a celery stick. Let's be honest: Sags can be show-offs occasionally—but who can blame them? These fire signs are clever, well traveled, and knowledgeable! They will love this brunch variant, so don't be surprised if the Caesar becomes the go-to drink for worldly Sagittarians!

Caipirinha

Sagittarians are the wanderers of the zodiac. These fiery archers are on a constant quest for knowledge, so they seize every opportunity to travel and explore. But even when Sagittarians are forced to remain stationary, these curious fire signs will always find a way to discover something new and exciting. Whether they're parading through the Carnival of Brazil or simply couch-surfing, Sagittarians will love sipping Caipirinha cocktails. The national drink of Brazil, the Caipirinha's primary ingredient is cachaça—a Brazilian spirit derived from fermented sugarcane juice. The flavor of cachaça, when combined with muddled lime and sugar, is smooth, refreshing, and punchy. Sagittarians will love this delicious, South American concoction that makes the perfect companion for a warm summer night.

SERVES 1

2 teaspoons granulated sugar
Lime, wedged
2 ounces cachaça
Lime slice, seeded, for garnish

Add sugar and lime to a double old-fashioned glass and mix with a muddler or the base of a wooden spoon. Fill glass with ice, add cachaça, and stir briefly. Garnish with lime slice. Grab a feathered boa and throw on some sequins—let's get ready to samba!

Fountain of Youth

Sagittarius is ruled by Jupiter—the celestial body known to traditional astrologers as the "Greater Benefic" (as opposed to Venus, the "Lesser Benefic"). Generous Jupiter is associated with abundance and good fortune, so it's no surprise that Sagittarians often look younger than their age. For those fiery archers who want to turn back the clock even more, the Fountain of Youth cocktail is the perfect boozy potion. This revitalizing beverage combines prosecco, vodka, and elderflower liqueur with lemon juice to create a fabulously fizzy, herbal blend. Spry Sagittarians will adore this buoyant beverage that effortlessly mirrors their own ebullient dispositions.

SERVES 1

1½ ounces vodka

¾ ounce elderflower liqueur

¾ ounce lemon juice

2 ounces prosecco

2 fresh mint leaves, for garnish

Orange slice, seeded, for garnish

Combine all ingredients except prosecco and garnishes in a shaker filled with ice. Shake vigorously, and strain into a highball glass filled with crushed ice. Add prosecco, and garnish with mint leaves and orange slice—now drink in the sparkling, youthful vitality.

French Monaco

Jet-setting Sagittarians will adore the French Monaco. This light, elegant beverage combines amber beer, lemon-lime club soda, and grenadine to create a crisp and frothy afternoon treat. It's also distinctive in color: the grenadine provides a striking rosy hue, which makes this bubbly cocktail extra alluring. The charming French Monaco is the ideal summertime refreshment for Sagittarians looking to cool off in style. Though relatively unknown in the United States, these super sippable cocktails are popular throughout France. But be advised: ordering a French Monaco in France is akin to ordering a Shirley Temple mocktail in the United States. Though these beer-based beverages are considered "children's drinks," don't be dissuaded by the association: the French Monaco is so delicious, it's definitely worth any raised eyebrows.

SERVES 1

4 ounces amber beer
2 ounces lemon-lime club soda
¼ teaspoon grenadine

Combine beer, club soda, and grenadine in a highball glass and stir. Á votre santé!

Greyhound

Adventurous Sagittarians love to travel. These fire signs project their arrows into faraway lands, inspiring the passionate archers to go the distance. Whether by plane, train, automobile, or even cross-country bus, Sagittarians are always ready to begin a new quest. The Greyhound cocktail is a straightforward and classic drink that effortlessly blends vodka and grapefruit juice—two unassuming ingredients that create a delicious, citrusy refreshment. Efficient and direct, the Greyhound cocktail is quick and easy to prepare, making this the ideal beverage for Sagittarians on the move.

SERVES 1

1½ ounces vodka
Grapefruit juice to fill

Lime wedge, for garnish

Pour vodka into a Collins glass filled with ice. Top off with grapefruit juice, stir, and garnish with lime wedge. No matter where you end up, this delicious cocktail will make you feel right at home.

Horse's Neck

Sagittarians are symbolized by the centaur—an archer who is half human, half horse. This mythological figure represents Sagittarians' ability to seamlessly traverse both the spiritual and material worlds, employing animalistic bravery when needed to advance the centaur's emotional growth. Due to the rich folklore, Sagittarians are deeply connected to horses, so these fire signs will love the Horse's Neck cocktail. Though this beverage is extremely easy to prepare (it's simply whiskey and ginger ale), its defining feature is the presentation: a long strip of lemon peel draped over the side of the glass to represent a horse's neck. Sagittarians will adore this captivating, tasty beverage that evokes their celestial spirit animal.

SERVES 1

2 ounces whiskey
Ginger ale to fill
Long strip lemon peel, for garnish

Pour whiskey into a Collins glass filled with ice. Top off with ginger ale, and garnish with long strip of lemon peel. You'll definitely be feeling your oats after a few sips—so giddyup, Sagittarius, it's time to saddle up!

Mai Tai

The Mai Tai is arguably the most famous of the tiki-craze drinks. This delicious rum-based cocktail was created by Trader Vic—the American entrepreneur largely responsible for propagating tiki culture—at his flagship Oakland bar in 1944. Trader Vic was experimenting with different tropical elixirs, and when he shared his most recent creation with a friend visiting from Tahiti, the beverage received resounding approval: *"Maita'i roa ae!"* (Tahitian for "The best!") Trader Vic shortened the expression for his concoction, and the rest is history. Sagittarians are natural storytellers, and these inspired fire signs will be sure to adore the Mai Tai's captivating origins—as well as the cocktail's perfectly balanced flavor profile.

SERVES 1

2 ounces dark rum
¾ ounce lime juice
½ ounce orange liqueur
¼ ounce rock candy syrup
¼ ounce orgeat liqueur
Fresh mint leaf, for garnish

Combine all ingredients except garnish in a shaker filled with crushed ice. Shake vigorously until the shaker is well chilled and frosty on the outside. Pour mixture (unstrained) into a double old-fashioned glass. Garnish with fresh mint leaf. *Maita'i roa ae!*

Manhattan

Tried and true, the Manhattan is one of the oldest cocktails. Invented in the mid-1800s, the Manhattan was one of the first drinks to incorporate vermouth, paving the way for future legends (such as the martini). Though its precise origins remain unknown, it is clear that the Manhattan reigned supreme by 1890. Over 150 years since its initial debut, the Manhattan maintains its regal title. This delicious and well-balanced cocktail is served worldwide and is considered one of the best cocktails ever created. Sagittarians will love the Manhattan's simplicity: containing only three ingredients, this beverage is easy to prepare and fun to perfect (it's often one of the first beverages that aspiring bartenders practice). Fiery archers will appreciate the Manhattan's rich history and relish the opportunity to pass down this time-honored cocktail.

SERVES 1

2 ounces rye whiskey
1 ounce sweet vermouth

5 drops bitters
Maraschino cherry, for garnish

Chill a martini glass in the freezer for five minutes. Combine all ingredients except garnish in a mixing glass filled with ice and stir. Strain into chilled martini glass, and garnish with maraschino cherry. New York is considered the "Capital of the World," and after tasting this cocktail, you'll understand why Manhattan has earned its prestigious reputation.

Matador

Courageous and thrill-seeking, Sagittarians are aren't afraid to grab life by the horns. Though Sagittarians don't *intend* to cause trouble, their curiosity often steers them into tricky situations. It wouldn't be surprising, for instance, for a Sagittarius traveling through Spain to inadvertently find herself in the center of an active bullring. Yikes! As an equally exciting (but a lot less risky) alternative, Sagittarians should consider sipping the Matador cocktail. This zesty refreshment blends gold tequila, pineapple juice, and lime juice to create a dynamic flavor combination that will be sure to quell Sagittarians' insatiable mischievousness...well, at least temporarily.

SERVES 1

1½ ounces gold tequila
3 ounces pineapple juice
½ ounce lime juice

Combine all ingredients in a shaker filled with ice. Strain into an old-fashioned glass filled with fresh ice. Olé!

Moscow Mule

Over the years, various mixologists, marketers, and even bar patrons have claimed responsibility for the creation of the Moscow Mule. Though it's difficult to discern fact from fiction, one thing is clear: the Moscow Mule never goes out of style. In addition to the refreshing combination of vodka and ginger beer, the Moscow Mule's defining feature is its clever copper mug that keeps the beverage cool. Sagittarians will love the distinctive look and feel of this tangy classic.

SERVES 1

3 ounces ginger beer
2 ounces vodka
Juice of one half lime
1 lime slice, seeded, for garnish

Combine all ingredients except garnish in a copper Moscow Mule mug filled with ice. Garnish with lime slice. Lean into the attention and enjoy!

Panama

Though exploratory Sagittarians would prefer to visit the country itself, the Panama cocktail is the next best thing. Equal parts white crème de cacao, brandy, and cream, the Panama's unique flavor makes this libation extremely versatile: it can be enjoyed as a pre-dinner aperitif, a post-dinner palate quencher, or a late-night pick-me-up. However fiery archers choose to sip the Panama, they will be sure to fall in love with this delicious and playful cocktail.

SERVES 1

1 ounce white crème de cacao
1 ounce brandy
1 ounce heavy cream

Chill a martini glass in the freezer for five minutes. Combine all ingredients in a shaker filled with ice. Shake, and strain the mixture into chilled martini glass.

Pisco Sour

Worldly Sagittarians will adore the Pisco Sour. Now considered a South American classic, this tangy cocktail was invented around 1920 at a high-society saloon in Lima, Peru. The beverage's primary ingredient is pisco—a brandy produced in the winemaking regions of Peru and Chile. Pisco's naturally sweet, fruity flavor is enhanced by simple syrup and lime juice, while a shaken egg white produces a silky texture and frothy head that is topped with bitters. Sagittarians will adore this delicious cocktail that is defined by its bright, citrusy blend.

SERVES 1

2 ounces pisco
1 ounce lime juice
½ ounce simple syrup

1 egg white
Lime slice, seeded, for garnish
3 drops bitters, for garnish

Combine all ingredients except garnishes in a shaker filled with ice. Shake extremely vigorously, and strain into a highball glass. Garnish with lime slice and bitters. Bitters will settle in the foam of the beverage. If you're feeling inspired, use a straw to swirl the bitters into a simple design.

Sidecar

Thrill-seeking Sagittarians are always pursuing adventure. Whether paddling down the Amazon River, scaling the side of Mount Kilimanjaro, or snowshoeing across Sun Valley, these passionate archers thrive on adrenaline. The classic Sidecar is the perfect cocktail for fearless Sagittarians. Invented in the 1920s, this brandy-based beverage was named after the now-vintage motorcycle attachment. An elegant combination of cognac, orange liqueur, and lemon juice, the Sidecar has been delivering a delicate, well-balanced flavor profile for almost a century. Its defining feature, however, is in the sugar-rimmed martini glass, which punctuates each sip with irresistible sweetness.

SERVES 1

Granulated sugar

½ orange

1½ ounces cognac

¾ ounce orange liqueur

¾ ounce lemon juice

Orange peel, for garnish

Run orange along the rim of a martini glass, then dip the glass in a saucer of sugar. Set glass aside. Combine remaining ingredients except garnish in a shaker filled with ice. Shake, and strain into prepared glass. Garnish with orange peel, a pair of aviator sunglasses, and your favorite shearling bomber jacket. Hey, the vintage look is timeless!

Capricorn

(DECEMBER 22–JANUARY 19): THE BOSS

Capricorns are the last earth sign of the zodiac, represented by the sea goat: a mythological creature with the upper body of a goat and the lower body of a fish. The elusive sea goat can navigate both the land and ocean, symbolizing Capricorns' innate ability to seamlessly engage both logic and intuition. Not to mention sea goats always put their skills to good use: Capricorn is the most ambitious sign of the zodiac. Capricorns are ruled by Saturn—the planet that governs discipline and painstaking lessons—so these illustrious earth signs know that success requires diligent hard work. Capricorns always have a five-year plan, and these tenacious sea goats aren't afraid to climb the ladder straight to the top. After a long day's work, however, Capricorns are delighted to let loose with their closest confidants. These earth signs value quality time with their friends and lovers, and enjoy building a community with like-minded companions.

Capricorns take their drinks seriously. There is *nothing* these earth signs despise more than flowery, neon-colored beverages garnished with superfluous miniature umbrellas. Capricorns' cocktails demand respect. These sea goats choose time-honored libations, like the classic Old-Fashioned, the Vesper cocktail (made popular by James Bond, no less), and the iconic Brandy Alexander. Whichever cocktails Capricorns select, they will be sure to match these sea goats' esteemed reputation.

1870 Sour

The 1870 Sour is an unexpected cocktail that is the perfect choice for pioneering Capricorns. Though a modern variant of the timeless Whiskey Sour, this beverage's catchy name has historical significance: the Whiskey Sour was first mentioned in a Wisconsin newspaper in 1870. The 1870 Sour builds on the traditional cocktail by adding lemon juice, blueberry jam, and maple syrup to the whiskey-and-egg-white blend. While these ingredients are not often included in cocktails, their traditional flavors delicately enhance the frothy sour mixture. For a final touch of elegance, red wine is floated to the top of the drink, creating a vivid rosy hue. Capricorns will love this contemporary cocktail that pays homage to its heritage.

SERVES 1

2 ounces whiskey
1 ounce lemon juice
¾ ounce maple syrup

1 teaspoon blueberry jam
1 egg white
1 ounce sweet red wine

Chill a mason jar glass in the freezer for five minutes. Combine all ingredients except wine in a shaker. Shake vigorously for ten seconds, then fill shaker with ice and shake for an additional fifteen seconds. Fine-strain into chilled mason jar, floating the wine by gently pouring it over the back of a spoon into the drink.

Black and Tan

The Black and Tan is the perfect choice for clever Capricorns. This classic beer-based cocktail combines two completely different brews in a single glass. While this mixture may sound odd, the art of blending beers is actually a long-established tradition: English drinkers have been mixing brews since the 1600s. This particular concoction—which combines pale ale and stout—has been enjoyed in the United Kingdom since the late 1800s. Capricorns will adore this practical cocktail that employs basic physics: the denser liquid (stout) is gently layered on top of the lighter liquid (pale ale), creating a strikingly divided beverage.

SERVES 1

6 ounces pale ale beer
6 ounces stout beer

Fill a pint glass halfway with pale ale. Float the stout on top by slowly pouring it over the back of a spoon to fill the glass. Note: travelers should avoid ordering this beverage by name in Ireland, as "Black and Tan" was the nickname for the English nationals who violently resisted the Irish independence. Instead, drinkers should order a "Half and Half."

Bloodhound

Despite its ferocious name, the Bloodhound is nothing to fear. In fact, the Bloodhound has been a cocktail favorite for over one hundred years—early iterations of this classic libation date back to 1917. This crimson martini combines gin, sweet vermouth, dry vermouth, and strawberry liqueur to create a perfectly well-balanced, potent concoction. Capricorns—the last earth sign of the zodiac—are disciplined traditionalists who enjoy honoring historical conventions and multigenerational legacies. Naturally, these practical sea goats will adore the Bloodhound, the timeless creation that has enchanted mixologists and alcohol enthusiasts for generations.

SERVES 1

1 ounce gin
½ ounce sweet vermouth
½ ounce dry vermouth

½ ounce strawberry liqueur
Fresh strawberry, for garnish

Combine all ingredients except garnish in a cocktail shaker filled with ice. Shake vigorously for thirty seconds until cold, then strain the mixture into a martini glass. Garnish with fresh strawberry. A few sips of this is guaranteed to make even the tamest Capricorn howl—enjoy!

Brandy Alexander

The Brandy Alexander is a timeless favorite that has a long-standing place in cultural history. In fact, the Brandy Alexander is a bit of a celebrity: this cocktail has landed starring roles in multiple films and novels throughout the twentieth century. This glamorous concoction combines cognac, dark crème de cacao, and heavy cream to create a rich, luxurious flavor. The Brandy Alexander's subtle chocolate essence and velvety finish make this cocktail the perfect after-dinner treat to be enjoyed as a decadent, boozy dessert. Capricorns will love this sensual beverage that evokes the classic elegance of bygone eras.

SERVES 1

2 ounces cognac
1 ounce dark crème de cacao

1 ounce heavy cream
Dash ground nutmeg, for garnish

Chill a martini glass in the freezer for five minutes. Combine all ingredients except garnish in a cocktail shaker filled with ice. Shake well, then strain into chilled martini glass. Garnish with ground nutmeg. This timeless classic may quickly become Capricorn's go-to beverage for warming up on cold, wintry nights.

Brass Monkey

In many ways, the Brass Monkey's name is more famous than the beverage itself. The Beastie Boys rapped about this combination of vodka, light rum, and orange juice in their 1987 hit of the same name, but many listeners had misconceptions about the beverage, believing the song referenced a completely different concoction (40-ounce malt liquor and orange juice). Capricorns value accuracy, and these straightforward sea goats will love to finally set the record straight. Easy to prepare, enjoy, and clarify, the punchy Brass Monkey is the ideal drink for Capricorns who *hate* misunderstandings.

SERVES 1

5 ounces orange juice

1 ounce light rum

1 ounce vodka

Orange wedge, for garnish

Combine all ingredients except garnish in shaker filled with ice and shake until mixture is cold. Strain, pouring into a Collins glass filled with fresh ice. Garnish with orange wedge, boom box, and neon track suit for a complete "funky monkey" experience.

Espresso Martini

The Espresso Martini is a perfect after-dinner pick-me-up that Capricorns will adore. This creamy, caffeinated concoction was created by legendary London-based mixologist Dick Bradsell while working at the Soho Brasserie. When a famous patron (rumored to be supermodel Kate Moss) asked for a drink that would wake them up, and then mess them up, Bradsell went to work. His innovative solution was a combination of vodka, freshly brewed espresso, coffee liqueur, and simple syrup—a deliciously well-blended cocktail that packs a punch. Illustrious sea goats will be sure to love this stimulating refreshment...after all, Kate Moss is a Capricorn.

SERVES 1

2 ounces vodka
1 ounce freshly brewed espresso
½ ounce simple syrup

½ ounce coffee liqueur
3 coffee beans, for garnish

Chill a martini glass in the freezer for five minutes. Combine all ingredients except garnish in a shaker filled with ice. Shake, and fine-strain the mixture into chilled martini glass. Garnish with three coffee beans. Be careful: this combination can certainly pack a punch, so sip slowly to avoid any tabloid-worthy drama!

Godfather

Capricorn symbolizes the father, making the Godfather a perfect drink for this parental sign. Comprising only two ingredients— scotch and amaretto—the Godfather is easy to prepare. This straightforward blend creates a rich and smooth flavor that earthy Capricorns will adore. Whether sipped during happy hour or as an after-dinner digestif, the Godfather will channel Capricorn's inner Don Corleone.

SERVES 1

2 ounces blended scotch
¼ ounce amaretto

Combine all ingredients in a mixing glass filled two-thirds of the way with ice, and stir until chilled. Strain into a rocks glass filled with fresh ice. Now *that's* an offer no one can refuse.

Irish Coffee

Capricorn is the most ambitious sign of the zodiac, so it's no surprise that illustrious sea goats enjoy Irish Coffee. This clever blend is more complex than pouring whiskey over hot coffee: great Irish Coffee requires skill and finesse. A well-balanced Irish Coffee adds warmth to a cold evening, as well as inspiration when Capricorns are burning the midnight oil.

SERVES 1

Hot water
1½ ounces whiskey
1 ounce brown sugar syrup
Freshly brewed coffee
Whipped cream, for garnish

Preheat an Irish coffee glass by filling with hot water. Let sit for two minutes, then discard water. Pour whiskey and syrup into glass and top off with coffee. For a special treat, garnish with whipped cream.

Jaded Lady

Capricorns are the last earth sign of the zodiac, so these knowing sea goats have truly seen it all before. It takes a lot to impress Capricorns, but one cocktail that will be sure to dazzle even the most disillusioned sea goats is the Jaded Lady. This vibrant cocktail combines gin, advocaat liqueur (a rich spirit made from eggs, sugar, and brandy), orange juice, and blue curaçao to create a distinctive flavor and appearance. This beverage is tangy, creamy, and eye-catching (when poured carefully, the blue curaçao sinks to the bottom of the drink, creating an electrifying pop of color); Capricorns will become instantly enchanted by the Jaded Lady.

SERVES 1

1½ ounces gin
1½ ounces advocaat liqueur
½ ounce orange juice
⅛ ounce blue curaçao
Dash bitters

Chill a martini glass in the freezer for five minutes. Combine all ingredients except blue curaçao in a shaker filled with ice. Shake, and fine-strain into chilled martini glass. Carefully pour blue curaçao through the center of the drink, allowing liqueur to sink to the bottom. This vivid libation is far from blasé—enjoy, dear Capricorn!

Juan Collins

Capricorns will know there is a definite draw of these stoic sea goats to tequila. Astrologers believe that sea goats are drawn to the agave-derived spirit because it's a natural mood enhancer, and Capricorns (ruled by unflappable Saturn) are always seeking a pick-me-up. These earth signs will love the Juan Collins—the tequila version of the classic gin-based Tom Collins. The Juan Collins combines tequila with club soda, lemon juice, and agave nectar, creating a refreshingly sweet and tangy blend that is guaranteed to uplift even the most saturnine sea goats.

SERVES 1

1½ ounces silver tequila
1 ounce lemon juice
½ ounce agave nectar

2 ounces club soda
Lemon wedge, for garnish

Combine tequila, lemon juice, and agave nectar in a Collins glass filled with ice. Stir thoroughly, and add club soda. Garnish with lemon wedge. After a few sips, Capricorns will know why this drink is the most exuberant member of the Collins cocktail family.

London Fog

The city of London mirrors many of Capricorns' most quintessential attributes: like these sea goats, London values tradition and the spirit of entrepreneurship, and has demonstrated relentless resilience. The London Fog is a simple cocktail with an irresistible flavor and alluring presentation that Capricorns will love. Comprising only gin and pastis (an anise-flavored liqueur that has a distinct licorice taste), the London Fog is a straightforward refreshment that's easy to prepare. The combination of these two ingredients yields an aromatic and herbal flavor, while the pastis's opacity creates a reddish-orange, cloudy appearance that perfectly captures the misty atmosphere of London.

SERVES 1

1½ ounces gin
¼ ounce pastis

Chill a martini glass in the freezer for five minutes. Combine ingredients in a cocktail shaker filled with ice, and stir for thirty seconds. Strain into chilled martini glass.

Mezcal Margarita

The traditional Margarita cocktail features tequila, but Capricorns will love the mezcal-based variant. Though tequila and mezcal are both extracted from agave plants, the two spirits are distinct: while tequila is made exclusively from the blue agave plant and baked in an above-ground oven, mezcal can be created from any agave plant (there are over twenty varieties) and is prepared in a subterranean pit. Though there are many notable differences between these two Mexican alcohols, the most obvious is the taste. Capricorns will enjoy mezcal's signature smoky flavor, which adds a wonderfully earthy base to the classic, tangy Margarita cocktail.

SERVES 1

½ lime
Kosher salt
1½ ounces mezcal

¾ ounce lime juice
1 ounce orange liqueur
Lime wedge, for garnish

Run lime over the rim of a rocks glass, and dip the rim in a saucer of salt. Combine mezcal (watch out for the larva at the bottom of the bottle!), lime juice, and orange liqueur into a shaker filled with ice, and shake vigorously. Fill prepared glass with fresh ice, and pour in the mixture. Garnish with lime wedge.

Old-Fashioned

Dignified and delicious, there is no cocktail as esteemed as the Old-Fashioned. The first written reference of the word "cocktail" was in 1806, when a magazine editor defined the term as a potent concoction of spirits, bitters, waters, and sugar. Over the next several decades, alcoholic beverages became increasingly popular and began featuring fragrant liqueurs such as orange curaçao and absinthe. By the 1860s, cocktails had become so ornate that there was a strong movement to return to the basics—the "Old-Fashioned" recipe. Capricorns will adore this quintessential cocktail that epitomizes elegant simplicity.

SERVES 1

1 teaspoon granulated sugar
4 dashes bitters
Splash club soda
2 orange slices, seeded and divided
2 sour cherries, divided
2 ounces bourbon

In an old-fashioned glass, use a muddler or the base of a wooden spoon to muddle sugar, bitters, club soda, one orange slice, and one cherry. Remove orange rind, fill glass with ice, and add bourbon. Garnish with remaining orange slice and cherry. Drink slowly to relish the look and feel of this pioneering cocktail that never goes out of style.

Saturn

Capricorns are ruled by the planet Saturn, so it's no surprise that these sea goats will adore the island-inspired cocktail that derived its name from this powerful celestial body. The Saturn cocktail was created in 1967, and redefined the tiki composition by using gin (as opposed to rum) as its alcohol base. A fruity and floral combination of juices (lemon and passion fruit) and liqueurs (orgeat and falernum), the refreshing Saturn cocktail is the perfect companion for hot summer days. Though its vibrant flavors are significantly more upbeat than its astrological namesake (the planet Saturn can be a bit of a downer), Capricorns will enjoy this tasty, tropical classic that is truly out of this world.

SERVES 1

1¼ ounces gin
½ ounce lemon juice
½ ounce passion fruit syrup
¼ ounce orgeat liqueur
½ ounce falernum liqueur
Edible squash blossom, for garnish
Orange peel, for garnish

Combine all ingredients except garnishes in a blender filled with crushed ice and blend until smooth. Pour unstrained into a tiki mug, garnishing with edible flower, orange peel, and straw.

Screwdriver

Capricorns are straightforward and direct. These hardworking earth signs do not want to waste their precious time concocting ostentatious, elaborate beverages, so they prefer uncomplicated cocktails that are effortlessly delicious. The Screwdriver is the perfect refreshment for candid Capricorns. There are no mysteries, no surprises, and no pretensions with this classic refreshment: the ingredients are just vodka and orange juice. This naturally tasty, no-frills combination has been satisfying drinkers for generations, boasting a light and citrusy flavor that's perfect for any time of day. Capricorns will adore this easy-to-prepare cocktail that is respected for its seamless simplicity.

SERVES 1

1½ ounces vodka
Orange juice to fill

Add vodka to a highball glass filled with ice, and top off with orange juice. Rumor has it, this delicious drink was named after workers—lacking a spoon—decided to mix it with a screwdriver. Though we don't *necessarily* recommend this technique, after a few sips, Capricorns will understand the extreme measure: this concoction is just too delicious to forgo!

Vesper

Known by his code—007—James Bond is an elusive secret agent who defines the essence of cool. But perhaps Bond's most mysterious attribute is his ambiguous zodiac sign; Ian Fleming, the author of the James Bond series, never revealed the protagonist's date of birth. Though the astrological community can only speculate on 007's birth chart, Capricorns will enjoy creating their own Bond by sipping Fleming's original alcoholic creation: the Vesper cocktail. First featured in the 1953 novel *Casino Royale*, the Vesper is an elegant mixture of gin, vodka, and vermouth garnished with a lemon peel. Capricorns will love this delicious 007 classic that always delivers a stylish appearance and smooth taste... with a hint of danger.

SERVES 1

3 ounces gin
1 ounce vodka

½ ounce dry vermouth
Lemon peel, for garnish

James Bond's character invented the Vesper, so he delivered very specific instructions to the bartender when ordering the cocktail in *Casino Royale*. Summarizing his directions: chill a martini glass in the freezer for five minutes. Combine all ingredients except garnish in a mixing glass filled with ice. Stir and strain into chilled martini glass. Twist lemon peel around the drink, rubbing peel along the rim of the glass, and then drop it in the drink.

Aquarius

(JANUARY 20–FEBRUARY 18): THE REVOLUTIONARY

Aquarius, the last air sign of the zodiac, is actually symbolized by the water bearer: the generous healer who bestows life (water) upon the land. Likewise, Aquarius is the most humanitarian sign of the zodiac, fervently supporting power to the people. These water bearers are freethinkers who aspire to benefit the greater good through radical social change. Because Aquarians are most impassioned by the spirit of egalitarianism, this air sign advocates teamwork by participating in communities of like-minded progressives.

Aquarius is ruled by Uranus (the planet that governs rebellion and innovation), making these air signs unconventional, defiant, and eccentric. Aquarians *hate* uniformity, so these water bearers can often be spotted by their offbeat fashion, unusual hobbies, and nonconformist attitude. It comes as no surprise then that when it comes to libations, Aquarians aren't afraid to think outside the box. These water bearers enjoy cocktails that mirror the air sign's unconventionality by putting a new twist on old favorites. Aquarians will love the quirky Beermosa, the rebooted Mexican Mule, and the progressive Cuba Libre. Aquarians are far from basic, so don't even bother serving this air sign a "normal" beverage. In fact, Aquarians may actually become *annoyed* if offered a simple American lager. Whether social, political, or just plain provocative, Aquarians will always choose cocktails that make a statement.

Agent Orange

While the Agent Orange cocktail features a delicious blend of bright and citrusy spirits (orange juice, vodka, and triple sec), its namesake recalls a very different concoction. Equal parts herbicide 2,4,5-T and 2,4-D were mixed to create a powerful toxin—better known as Agent Orange. This extremely toxic chemical was used during the Vietnam War's herbicidal warfare program, which caused both major environmental damage as well as serious health problems to those exposed. Aquarius is the most politically minded sign of the zodiac, and Aquarians are always seeking platforms that spark meaningful conversation. These humanitarian air signs will appreciate this deliciously provocative cocktail that will be sure to stir the pot.

SERVES 1

2 ounces orange juice

1 ounce vodka

1 ounce triple sec

Orange slice, seeded, for garnish

Chill a rocks glass in the freezer for five minutes. Combine all ingredients except garnish in a shaker filled with ice. Shake, and strain into chilled rocks glass filled with fresh ice. Garnish with an orange slice. This cocktail's namesake may be dangerous, but the drink is absolutely delicious.

Bananarita

Boasting the flavor of a Frozen Banana Daiquiri and the spirit of a Frozen Margarita, the Bananarita is a playful, delicious, and potent concoction that Aquarians will adore. The Bananarita blends tequila, banana liqueur, pineapple juice, and cream to create a rich, velvety fusion defined by its fruity and tropical tang. Epitomizing the spirit of experimentation that defines mixology, Aquarians will appreciate this concoction's lighthearted unconventionality. Original, inventive, and fun to both prepare and sip, the Bananarita is a terrific companion for quirky Aquarians who always admire clever ingenuity.

SERVES 1

2 ounces heavy cream
1 ounce banana liqueur
1 ounce silver tequila

1 ounce pineapple juice
1½ teaspoons granulated sugar
Maraschino cherry, for garnish

Combine all ingredients except garnish in a blender filled with ice, mixing until smooth. Pour into a margarita glass, and garnish with maraschino cherry. Aquarians will go bananas for this delicious, frosted treat!

Beermosa

Aquarians *hate* being told what to do. These air signs are rebels at heart, and are guided by their insatiable desire to break the rules. Conventions? Toss 'em. Traditions? Forget it. Aquarians have no patience for antiquated systems, which they firmly believe delay forward motion. Alternatively, however, Aquarians are drawn to anything eccentric or innovative, making the quirky Beermosa the perfect beverage for these intellectual revolutionaries. The Beermosa replaces champagne with Mexican beer, fusing the light brew's crispy effervescence with the citrus flavors of orange juice. Buoyant, bright, and appropriately defiant, this progressive alternative to the go-to brunch favorite will be loved by Aquarians.

SERVES 1

2 ounces orange juice
12 ounces Mexican beer

Combine ingredients in a champagne flute and propose a toast to innovation!

Bloody Maria

The Bloody Maria is more than just a tequila-based version of the Bloody Mary: it's a complete game changer. Unlike vodka (the base of traditional Bloody Marys), which becomes absorbed by the cocktail's other ingredients, the tequila in a Bloody Maria maintains its prominent presence. When blended with the tomato juice, the savory notes of the agave-based alcohol create a completely new flavor profile, rich with vegetal earthiness. The Bloody Maria's characteristic accoutrements also reflect this spirited adaptation, further enhancing the beverage through two types of hot sauce (Tabasco and Tapatio), as well as a jalapeño slice for garnish. Creative Aquarians will love this complete cocktail makeover that is guaranteed to add some serious spice to brunch.

SERVES 1

4 ounces tomato juice
2 ounces gold tequila
½ ounce lemon juice
4 dashes Worcestershire sauce
2 dashes Tabasco sauce
2 dashes Tapatio hot sauce
Pinch celery salt
Pinch ground black pepper
Lime wedge, for garnish
Lemon wedge, for garnish
Cucumber spear, for garnish
Jalapeño slice, seeded, for garnish

Combine all ingredients except garnishes in a shaker filled with ice. Shake briefly, and strain into a pint glass filled with fresh ice. Garnish with lime wedge, lemon wedge, cucumber spear, and jalapeño slice. At last, a new take on an old favorite!

Cousin Vitamine

Aquarians are inventive and eccentric. While most signs prefer sipping established cocktails that boast time-honored legacies, Aquarians are inspired by new and unusual concoctions. The original Cousin Vitamine is the perfect cocktail for trailblazing Aquarians. This vodka-based beverage blends peach syrup with orange juice and cranberry juice, producing a stunning coral hue and a delicious, well-balanced tropical flavor. But while the combination of ingredients is recognizable, the drink itself is relatively unknown. In fact, the Cousin Vitamine is a completely new beverage (earliest references date back to 2013), providing Aquarians with the unique opportunity to define the spirit of this cocktail. With a completely blank slate, the Cousin Vitamine may very well become Aquarians' signature drink.

SERVES 1

2 ounces cranberry juice
2 ounces orange juice
1 ounce vodka
½ ounce peach syrup
Orange slice, seeded, for garnish

Combine all ingredients except garnish in a rocks glass filled with ice. Garnish with orange slice. Unlike most cocktails, this drink isn't embedded in the past—so cheers to a bright future, sweet Aquarian!

Cuba Libre

The revolution will not be televised...it will be sipped. Comprising only rum, cola, and lime juice, the Cuba Libre is a simple cocktail with a big message. The current iteration of the Cuba Libre was invented around the turn of the twentieth century: the United States had a large presence in Cuba following the Spanish-American War, which led to an increase of American imports into the newly independent Caribbean nation. The first shipment of Coca-Cola was received in 1900 and quickly inspired the creation of the Cuba Libre cocktail. Seditious Aquarians will love the passion that defines this beverage. Refreshing, zesty, and pioneering, these air signs will adore the mighty beverage that served an important role in Cuban history.

SERVES 1

3 ounces cola
1 ounce white rum

½ ounce lime juice
Lime wedge, for garnish

Combine all ingredients except garnish in a highball glass filled with ice. Garnish with lime wedge and *viva la revolución*!

Gin Rickey

Let's face it—Aquarians enjoy proving people wrong. In fact, debunking is one of their favorite pastimes. This summer, Aquarians will love sipping on the Gin Rickey—a classic gin-based cocktail defined by its zesty fizz. Though in appearance the Gin Rickey resembles a Gin and Tonic (another traditional warm-weather favorite), the Gin Rickey has a unique history of its own. After a particularly brutal heat wave, the Gin Rickey was invented at Shoemaker's Saloon in Washington, DC, in the 1890s. The drink was concocted specifically to provide maximum cooling effects, distinguishing it from the Gin and Tonic, which was initially created to prevent malaria. Aquarians will love this delicious cocktail that is served with an unexpected narrative.

SERVES 1

1½ ounces gin
Lime, halved

Club soda to fill

Is the heat getting to you? Add gin to a highball glass filled with ice. Juice lime halves into the glass, and drop in the pulp and rinds. Top off with club soda.

Green Hornet

The Green Hornet is a fictional masked crime-fighter who's had a pervasive presence in American pop culture. The legendary vigilante debuted on January 31, 1936, (during Aquarius season) as a radio drama on a local station in Detroit. The Green Hornet's popularity quickly skyrocketed and has since expanded to comic books, television shows, and feature films. Aquarius is associated with large-scale movements, and in the teachings of modern astrology, the sign is believed to govern broadcasting, technology, and mass media. Aquarians will love the historic Green Hornet, along with the delicious cocktail that shares its name. The potent drink blends vodka, banana liqueur, absinthe, and lime juice to produce a distinctive tang that's the perfect companion for any adventure.

SERVES 1

¾ ounce vodka

¾ ounce banana liqueur

½ ounce lime juice

⅛ ounce absinthe

Quick, Kato—to the bar! Chill a shot glass in the freezer for five minutes. Combine all ingredients in a shaker filled with ice and shake well. Fine-strain mixture into chilled shot glass.

Italian Mojito

Aquarians will adore the Italian Mojito—an innovative take on the popular Cuban refreshment. Basil leaves are muddled with the traditional mint leaves, offsetting the cocktail's characteristic sweetness by adding compelling spicy and savory notes. Though the Italian Mojito maintains its classic rum base, a splash of prosecco (an Italian sparkling wine) is added to create a charming effervescence. Progressive Aquarians value modernization and advancements; on principle alone, these air signs will love the Italian Mojito's ingenuity, but after a few sips of this delicious beverage, Aquarians will be ready to float down a Venetian canal.

SERVES 1

5 fresh basil leaves, torn
5 fresh mint leaves, torn
1 ounce lime juice

1½ ounces light rum
Dash simple syrup
Splash prosecco

Using a muddler or the base of a wooden spoon, muddle mint and basil in a shaker. Fill shaker with ice and add rum, lime juice, and simple syrup. Shake vigorously, and strain into a highball glass. Add prosecco. *Bellissimo!*

John Collins

The eldest of the Collins cocktail family, the John Collins has undergone several transformations since its initial inception. Invented in the early 1800s by a headwaiter at a London coffeehouse of the same name, the John Collins was originally a gin-based cocktail. The name "Tom" replaced "John" in the late 1800s, however, after a popular recipe book misattributed the name. Today, the John Collins denotes the whiskey variation. Bourbon whiskey is combined with lemon juice, simple syrup, and club soda to create a sweet and citrusy refreshment. Aquarians will love the John Collins's bright buoyancy, as well as its eccentric history.

SERVES 1

1½ ounces bourbon whiskey
1 ounce lemon juice
½ ounce simple syrup

2 ounces club soda
Orange slice, seeded, for garnish
Maraschino cherry, for garnish

Combine all ingredients except club soda and garnishes in a Collins glass filled with ice. Stir thoroughly, and top with club soda. Garnish with orange slice and maraschino cherry.

Libertine

Freethinking Aquarians don't conform to societal standards. These philosophical air signs reject rules and regulations, and are directed instead by their own conceptions of morals and ethics. By sixteenth-century standards, Aquarian ideologies would be perceived as "libertine." A term initially used to describe those who opposed accepted sociopolitical thought, defiant libertines were antiestablishment, anticlericalism, and driven by personal enjoyment. Naturally, Aquarians will love the Libertine cocktail. This subversive concoction combines three spirits (vodka, Green Chartreuse, and elderflower liqueur) with ginger beer and lime juice to create a striking reddish-orange hue that delivers an unapologetically vibrant tang. Delicious and distinctive, the Libertine cocktail is definitely something any Aquarian can endorse.

SERVES 1

1½ ounces lime-flavored vodka
¾ ounce Green Chartreuse
¾ ounce elderflower liqueur

½ ounce lime juice
1 ounce ginger beer
Lime wedge, for garnish

Combine all ingredients except ginger beer and garnish in a shaker filled with ice. Shake well, and fine-strain into an old-fashioned glass filled with ice. Add ginger beer and stir lightly. Garnish with lime wedge—and a manifesto for a complete philosophical experience.

Mexican Mule

Innovative Aquarians will adore this delicious cocktail that refashions the Moscow Mule by replacing vodka with tequila. While the classic combination of vodka and ginger beer is certainly refreshing, the cleverly titled Mexican Mule adds a new dimension to this timeless concoction. Both plant-based, the tequila and ginger beer seamlessly enhance each other's unique warm and spicy flavors, creating a distinctive tangy and aromatic fusion. The additions of lime juice and simple syrup deliver a delicately sweet, zesty blend that Aquarians will relish.

SERVES 1

1½ ounces Reposado tequila
¾ ounce lime juice
¼ ounce simple syrup
Ginger beer to fill
Lime wedge, for garnish

Combine tequila, lime juice, and simple syrup in a shaker filled with ice. Shake well, and strain into copper mug filled with ice. Top off with ginger beer, stirring lightly, and garnish with lime wedge. Serve with a straw. *Sabe bien!*

Snowball

Tired of the same old holiday cocktails? The Snowball is the perfect treat to spice up the cold winter months. A seasonal favorite in the United Kingdom, the Snowball's distinguishing ingredient is advocaat liqueur, a Dutch-based spirit derived from a creamy blend of brandy, egg yolks, and aromatic spices. Combined with lime juice and lemon soda, the Snowball mixes sparkling citrus notes with the rich liqueur, creating a distinctive and alluring flavor. Aquarians will love this delicious, zesty elixir that guarantees to build heat from the inside out.

SERVES 1

3½ ounces lemon soda
¾ ounce lime juice
2 ounces advocaat liqueur
Lime slice, seeded, for garnish

Combine lemon soda and lime juice in a Collins glass filled with ice. Add advocaat liqueur. Stir lightly to avoid losing any carbonation. Though the weather outside may be frightful, a few sips of this delicious concoction will feel like a warm, liquid embrace!

Tequini

Though often relegated to sweet, summery drinks, tequila is actually a very versatile spirit. Its smooth, earthy flavor is effortlessly enhanced by cocktail mixers, while simultaneously providing a fabulous neutral base that never overpowers. Delicious and dynamic, the Tequini is a terrific cocktail that is, quite simply, a tequila-based martini. The silver tequila seamlessly blends with the vermouth, creating a drier finish than usually expected from a tequila drink. Popular throughout the 1960s and 1970s, the Tequini is a fun and tasty alternative to the traditional martini. Aquarians will love this distinctive beverage that adds a new twist to the cocktail staple.

SERVES 1

2½ ounces silver tequila
½ ounce dry vermouth
Dash bitters
3 green olives, for garnish

Chill a martini glass in the freezer for five minutes. Combine all ingredients except garnish in a cocktail shaker filled with ice. Shake well, and strain into chilled martini glass. Skewer olives on a toothpick to garnish. Both delicious and seldom seen, this offbeat cocktail will become an Aquarian favorite!

Whiskey Sour

The Whiskey Sour perfectly mirrors Aquarius's rebellious spirit. Though the Whiskey Sour is a historic cocktail (the first documented recipe was published in 1870), this punchy libation has always boasted a defiant edge. Unlike other nineteenth-century drinks that appealed exclusively to high society, the Whiskey Sour was modeled after the maritime grogs of the 1700s. Sailors would drink citrus-infused elixirs ("sours") to combat waterborne disease. Since it is both easy to prepare (the Whiskey Sour contains only three ingredients) and to sip, Aquarians will love this delicious concoction that is inextricably linked to the seafaring experience.

SERVES 1

1½ ounces bourbon whiskey
¾ ounce lemon juice
¾ ounce simple syrup
Maraschino cherry, for garnish

Combine all ingredients except garnish in a shaker filled with ice. Shake, and strain into a rocks glass filled with fresh ice. Garnish with lime wedge and maraschino cherry. Anchors aweigh!

Zombie

The Zombie was invented in 1934 at Don the Beachcomber's, a legendary Los Angeles island-themed bar. Rumor has it that the cocktail was initially created to help a hungover customer get through a business meeting—a plan that backfired when the extremely potent concoction transformed the patron into a "zombie." This powerful yet deliciously fruity drink actually predated the tiki craze of the 1950s and was the most sought-after tropical cocktail for many years. But Don was extremely secretive about his creations. Since he referred to most of his ingredients in code, the original Zombie recipe eventually faded into obscurity. Passionate Aquarians will love this potent island treat, and, by continuing to experiment with this iconic creation, will be sure to bring the Zombie back to life.

SERVES 1

1½ ounces orange juice
1½ ounces passion fruit purée
1 ounce light rum
1 ounce dark rum
1 ounce orange liqueur
½ ounce lemon juice

½ ounce lime juice
¼ ounce grenadine
2 dashes bitters
Fresh mint leaf,
    for garnish
Seasonal fruit slices, for garnish

Combine all ingredients except garnishes in a cocktail shaker filled with ice. Shake well and strain into a hurricane glass filled with fresh ice. Garnish with mint leaf and seasonal fruit slices. Sip slowly, Aquarius: Zombies are strong, so make sure you don't get *too* scary!

Pisces

(FEBRUARY 19–MARCH 20): THE DREAMER

The last sign of the zodiac, Pisces is a water sign symbolized by two fish swimming in opposite directions. Pisces are often pulled between fantasy and reality: this sign is the most psychic and intuitive of the zodiac, and with *such* incredible empathy, this compassionate water sign can become swallowed by the nonmaterial realm. Neptune (Pisces' planetary ruler) governs creativity and illusion, encouraging these ethereal fish to explore the vastness of their imaginations. Pisces are gentle, kind, and artistic souls who are invigorated by dreams, music, and romance. These sensitive fish are enchanted by love, even finding their partners' most grating flaws beautiful. Pisces' bonds are always karmic, and any relationship with a Pisces friend or lover is guaranteed to usher a deep dive into the subconscious.

Naturally, fish love to drink. Pisces are known to have a bit of a wild side, and enjoy activating their spirituality through mind-altering experiences. Hypnotic cocktails that awaken the senses perfectly complement Pisces' otherworldliness. Pisces will slip into fantasy while sipping the Foaming Fairy and fall head over heels with the Love Potion #9. Never try to anchor a Pisces with logical, straightforward mixed drinks; Pisces are magical creatures, so basic beverages (like an uninspired whiskey and cola) will surely prompt these ethereal water signs to swim upstream. For these mystical fish, there is always a link between the mind, body, and spirit...even during happy hour.

Blackberry Sage Tequila Smash

Fruity, fragrant, and irresistibly mouthwatering, the Blackberry Sage Tequila Smash is a simple, delightful cocktail that Pisces will savor. The name reveals the refreshment's most distinctive ingredients, which are elegantly prepared to create a lovely aromatic blend. First, blackberries, sage, and sugar are muddled to release their juices and essential oils. When this purée is combined with the earthy savor of tequila and citrus tang of grapefruit juice, this cocktail produces a refined and delicious flavor profile. Dewy-eyed Pisces will be sure to adore this herbal beverage that is guaranteed to create an instantly enrapturing ambience.

SERVES 1

3 large blackberries
8 fresh sage leaves, divided
2 cane sugar cubes

2 ounces silver tequila
1 ounce fresh grapefruit juice

With a muddler or the base of a wooden spoon, muddle blackberries, sage leaves, and sugar cubes into a mixing glass. Fill with crushed ice and add tequila and grapefruit juice. Shake vigorously, then pour into a mason jar filled with ice. Garnish with one sage leaf. You'll be sure to fall in love with this divine, aromatic concoction—enjoy!

Broken Heart

Pisces are spiritual beings who connect with friends and lovers on a deep level. These sweet, sentimental water signs are enchanted by romance, so it's no surprise that dreamy fish are always falling in love. Of course, this endearing quality also makes Pisces more susceptible to broken hearts. The next time the bottom falls out, Pisces should plan to mix it up with a shaken Broken Heart cocktail! This delectable beverage includes muddled berries, lime juice, and two types of flavored vodka (vanilla and raspberry) to create a sweet, decadent flavor profile that will be sure to soothe even the most anguished fish. Hey, after two of these, you may not even remember who you're crying about.

SERVES 1

½ cup mixed berries
1 ounce raspberry-flavored vodka
1 ounce vanilla-flavored vodka
Splash lime juice
Splash simple syrup
Lime wedge, for garnish

Using a muddler or the back of a wooden spoon, muddle berries in a shaker. Fill shaker with ice. Combine all remaining ingredients except garnish in shaker. Shake well, and pour (unstrained) into a rocks glass. Garnish with lime wedge. Who knew heartbreak could be so tasty?

Foaming Fairy

Pisces will love the Foaming Fairy cocktail. This ethereal sign is always teetering between fantasy and reality, striving to balance the material and subconscious realms. A few sips of the Foaming Fairy, however, will escort Pisces into a world of enchantment. This hypnotic libation alludes to none other than the "green fairy" (*la fée verte*)—the literary nickname given to the controversial absinthe spirit. The Foaming Fairy mixes absinthe, gin, and lemon juice with egg whites to create a frothy, magical treat. Pisces will adore this elegant and iconic creation that is guaranteed to leave a bewitching impression.

SERVES 1

2 ounces gin
½ ounce lemon juice
½ ounce absinthe
1 egg white
Dash bitters, for garnish

Chill a cocktail glass in the freezer for five minutes. Combine gin, lemon juice, absinthe, and egg white in a cocktail shaker. Shake vigorously for thirty seconds. Fill the shaker two-thirds with ice, and shake again until frothy (approximately forty seconds). Use a cocktail strainer to pour the mixture into chilled cocktail glass. Wait for foam to rise, and place bitters on top for garnish.

Ginger Martini

The gingerroot has a time-honored history in many traditional medicine practices. Loaded with nutrients and bioactive compounds, ginger is one of the healthiest spices around. From past to present, ginger has been used to treat nausea, relieve muscle pain, and lower blood sugar and cholesterol. Ginger is also extremely delicious, endowed with a bright and peppery essence that provides the perfect flavor profile for a delectable cocktail. Warm and spicy, the vodka-based Ginger Martini is a terrific companion for a cold winter night. Spiritual Pisces will adore the Ginger Martini, which will be sure to both satisfy the senses and revitalize the soul.

SERVES 1

3 ounces vodka
½ ounce ginger liqueur
Splash lime juice
Thin slice fresh ginger, for garnish

Chill a martini glass in the freezer for five minutes. Combine all ingredients except garnish in shaker filled with ice. Shake vigorously, and strain into chilled martini glass. Garnish with thin slice of fresh ginger to enhance the cocktail's inherent soothing sensations.

Half Windsor

Pisces need to luxuriate. These water signs love lathering up the moisturizer, submerging in the bathtub, and zoning out with their favorite music. While Pisces certainly enjoy the hedonistic aspects of indulgence, the driving force is self-care. Since Pisces are such receptive and empathic souls, it's essential that they create individual space to exist exclusively within their own thoughts, feelings, and expressions. The Half Windsor is the perfect companion for Pisces' next dose of "me time." This vodka-based cocktail includes agave nectar, lime juice, and *lots* of cucumbers, which is basically a spa day in itself. Pisces will love this soothing and refreshing beverage that is guaranteed to increase inner peace.

SERVES 1

1½ ounces vodka
¾ ounce cucumber juice
½ ounce agave nectar
½ ounce lime juice
3 cucumber slices, for garnish

Combine all ingredients except garnish in a cocktail shaker filled with ice. Shake well, and strain over fresh ice in a rocks glass. Garnish with cucumbers. What could be better than some booze-infused R & R?

Hurricane

Pisces' ruling planet, Neptune, symbolizes all ocean activity—including hurricanes. Naturally, these water signs will love the Hurricane cocktail. Founded at New Orleans' legendary Pat O'Brien's Bar in the 1940s, the beverage was initially concocted as a way for the proprietor to get rid of his lower-quality rum. Enjoyed first by sailors, the drink quickly developed a following and has since become a staple of the Big Easy's French Quarter. Though sweet and tropical, this cocktail stays true to its original recipe by packing a serious punch. Pisces will love this potent refreshment that will be sure to cause some whirlwinds.

SERVES 1

2 ounces white rum

2 ounces dark rum

1 ounce lime juice

1 ounce orange juice

2 ounces passion fruit juice

½ ounce simple syrup

½ ounce grenadine

Orange slice, seeded, for garnish

Maraschino cherry, for garnish

Combine all ingredients except garnishes in shaker filled with ice. Shake vigorously. Strain into a hurricane glass filled with fresh ice. Garnish with orange slice and maraschino cherry. Sip slowly, sweet Pisces: you don't want to end up in the eye of the storm!

Lemon Drop

Named after the classic hard candy of the same name, the Lemon Drop cocktail is a fresh, sweet, and zesty beverage that sensual Pisces will adore. Created in the 1970s at a once-popular singles bar in San Francisco, the Lemon Drop was designed specifically to appeal to female patrons. The proprietor's idea was simple: develop beverages that attract women, and men will always follow. The Lemon Drop proved to be an instant success, and continues to be enjoyed—by all genders—to this day. Dreamy Pisces will be charmed by this playful concoction that is renowned for its tartness and striking presentation.

SERVES 1

1 drop lemon juice
Granulated sugar
2 ounces vodka
1 ounce simple syrup
1 ounce lemon juice
½ ounce triple sec
Lemon twist, for garnish

Rub the rim of a martini glass with a drop of lemon juice and dip into a saucer of sugar. Set glass aside. Combine ingredients except garnish in a shaker filled with ice. Shake, and strain into prepared martini glass. Garnish with lemon twist. After just one sip, Pisces may be tempted to drop everything and focus exclusively on this delicious beverage.

Love Potion #9

Pisces is arguably the most romantic sign of the zodiac—even Venus (the planet of love) is exalted in its sign. Pisces is symbolized by two fish swimming in opposite directions, yet attached through an invisible force. For these sentimental fish, every relationship feels karmic—like two connected souls finally coming home. Simply put, Pisces love to be in love. Love Potion #9 is the perfect match for Pisces' rapture. This delicious cocktail combines muddled blueberries, strawberries, and basil leaves with raspberry-flavored vodka, creating a dreamy, aromatic blend of herbal and fruity flavors. Mystical Pisces should serve this beverage to their crushes: after a few sips of enchanting Love Potion #9, anyone will be ready to fall head over heels.

SERVES 1

⅓ cup fresh blueberries
⅓ cup fresh strawberries, hulled
⅓ cup fresh basil leaves
1½ ounces raspberry-flavored vodka
Fresh basil leaf, for garnish

Using a muddler or the base of a wooden spoon, carefully muddle berries and basil leaves in a rocks glass. Fill glass with ice, stir in vodka, and garnish with a basil leaf. Abracadabra!

Mind Eraser

We've all had those nights we've wanted to forget. Whether we said the wrong thing or went home with the wrong person, we woke up the next day overwhelmed with embarrassment (hey, it happens—we're only human). For those times you just wished you could erase the whole night, now you can. Well, sort of. The Mind Eraser is the perfect, potent "hair of the dog" cocktail. Pisces will love this clever three-part concoction that mixes vodka, coffee liqueur, and club soda to provide a jolt of liquid confidence... and, if you're lucky, maybe temporary amnesia as well.

SERVES 1

3 ounces club soda
1 ounce vodka
1 ounce coffee liqueur

Combine all ingredients in a rocks glass filled with ice and stir gently. Wait, what?

Mojito

The Cuban-born Mojito is one of the most popular summertime refreshments. Light, bubbly, and aromatic, the Mojito has been a warm-weather staple for the past five hundred years. Though under a different name, the Mojito's key ingredients—rum, sugarcane, mint, and lime—were first combined to help sailors prevent and treat waterborne illnesses. Though this cocktail's function is much more recreational today, the same tropical ingredients are combined to create this zesty delight. A perfect companion for poolside hangs or beach vacations, Pisces will love this fresh, simple cocktail that captures the essence of vivacity.

SERVES 1

5 fresh mint leaves
¾ ounce simple syrup
¾ ounce lime juice
1½ ounces white rum
1½ ounces club soda
Fresh mint leaf, for garnish

Using a muddler or the base of a wooden spoon, muddle the mint in a shaker. Fill the shaker with ice and add simple syrup, lime juice, and rum. Shake vigorously and pour (unstrained) into a highball glass. Add club soda and garnish the Mojito with a mint leaf. Pisces will love escaping the daily grind with this tall glass of oasis.

Rose Berry Bliss

Generous and hospitable, these water signs are natural hosts and hostesses. The Rose Berry Bliss cocktail is the perfect choice to serve at Pisces' next summertime hang. Rosé is the base of this distinctive beverage, combining with pink lemonade to create a rich, stunning coral hue. Blueberries are also added to the concoction, providing deliciously fruity visual accents (as well as tasty treats). The defining ingredient in the Rose Berry Bliss cocktail, however, is the lemon-lime soda. The zesty carbonation elegantly enhances the fresh flavors, creating a dynamic effervescence that is guaranteed to brighten any occasion. Pisces will love preparing and sipping this classy beverage that is delicate, tangy, and flawless in presentation.

SERVES 8

1 (25-ounce) bottle rosé
10 ounces frozen blueberries
1 (15-ounce) can frozen pink lemonade
Lemon-lime soda to fill

Combine wine, frozen blueberries, and frozen pink lemonade in a large pitcher. Enhance flavors by placing mixture in the refrigerator for an hour. When ready to serve, pour into champagne flutes and top off with lemon-lime soda. Ahh, sweet bliss!

Sea Breeze

This water sign thrives by the ocean. Whether sailing into the sunset, surfing across the waves, or simply lying out by the shore, Pisces are drawn to the sea. The Sea Breeze, which effortlessly captures that distinctive maritime atmosphere, is the perfect cocktail for aquatic Pisces. Containing only three ingredients—vodka, cranberry juice, and grapefruit juice—with no shakers required, this beverage is extremely easy to prepare. Cranberry and grapefruit juices blend seamlessly, delivering a smooth, tart flavor. Pisces will love this timeless refreshment that instantly transforms any afternoon into a nautical adventure.

SERVES 1

3 ounces cranberry juice
1½ ounces vodka
1½ ounces grapefruit juice
Lime slice, seeded, for garnish

Combine all ingredients except garnish in a highball glass filled with ice. Stir, and garnish with lime slice. Be sure to batten down the hatches: this tasty cocktail is often the gateway to a wild adventure!

Surfer on Acid

The Surfer on Acid is the perfect concoction for Pisces. Pisces is ruled by Neptune, the Roman god of the sea, and accordingly, modern astrologers connect all oceanic activities to Pisces, including sailing, rafting, snorkeling, and—you guessed it—surfing. Watery Pisces also symbolizes dreams, fantasies, and metaphysics, but on a bad day, Pisces represents escapism and delusion, linking the sign to hallucinogens. This bespoke shooter combines Jägermeister (a German digestif) with coconut rum and pineapple juice to create a delicious, beach-inspired blend that all Pisces—regardless of their hobbies—will be sure to enjoy.

SERVES 1

1 ounce Jägermeister
1 ounce coconut rum
Splash pineapple juice

Combine all ingredients in a cocktail mixer. Shake, and pour into a shot glass. Shoot, and follow the white rabbit.

Tom Collins

Today, the Tom Collins is the most popular drink of the Collins cocktail family, but it wasn't always that way. Invented by a London bartender of the same name in the mid-1800s, this gin-based beverage was originally titled John Collins. The John Collins recipe included "Old Tom Gin," which led to confusion surrounding the cocktail's title. By the late 1800s, the drink adopted the name Tom Collins, which is still associated with this refreshing, delicious, and straightforward cocktail. Pisces will enjoy sipping this historic refreshment to cool off on hot, balmy summer days. Light, zesty, and perfectly carbonated, it's no surprise that this drink has withstood the test of time.

SERVES 1

¾ ounce lemon juice

¾ ounce simple syrup

1½ ounces gin

Club soda to fill

Lemon slice, seeded, for garnish

Maraschino cherry, for garnish

Combine lemon juice, simple syrup, and gin in a cocktail shaker filled with ice. Shake well, and strain into a highball glass filled with fresh ice. Top off with club soda and garnish with a lemon slice and cherry. No need to run up your energy bill by blasting the AC: this delicious refreshment is guaranteed to keep you cool on even the hottest summer days.

Winter Warmer

Watery Pisces are extremely empathetic. These sensitive fish respond emotionally to everything from others' cranky moods to the atmospheric conditions of the season. Pisces adore cocktails that are perfectly paired with the time of year, and these delicate fish will enjoy getting cozy with the Winter Warmer. This simple refreshment blends vodka with honey and lemon juice to create a classic, soothing concoction guaranteed to keep Pisces warm with or without a fire. The combination of honey and lemon has been used historically to nurse sore throats and other winter ailments, so this tasty elixir has positive healing effects as well. Both delicious and restorative, the Winter Warmer is guaranteed to become one of Pisces' go-to cold-weather favorites.

SERVES 1

2 ounces vanilla vodka
1½ ounces honey
½ ounce lemon juice
2 ounces hot water

Combine all ingredients in an Irish coffee glass. Stir to mix flavors. Pisces will love bundling up with this cozy concoction!

Zen Tea Cocktail

Pisces is the most psychic sign of the zodiac. These ethereal fish are extremely sensitive creatures who are constantly absorbing surrounding energies—picking up on thoughts, feelings, and vibrations. All that clairvoyant exertion can be exhausting, so mystical Pisces will love chilling out with a Zen Tea Cocktail. This easy-to-prepare elixir combines vodka, brewed iced green tea, and freshly chopped ginger to create a soothing, verdant cocktail. Vodka's neutral flavor enhances the green tea's subtle, earthy tones, while the ginger adds a warm and spicy kick. After a few sips of this tranquil refreshment, Pisces will be sure to say, "*Namaste...* right here and finish my drink."

SERVES 1

3 ounces brewed iced green tea with sugar and lemon
2 ounces vodka
1 ounce chopped fresh ginger

First, take two big, restorative deep breaths. Transfer brewed iced green tea to glass pitcher, and cool in the refrigerator overnight. When ready to serve, chill a martini glass in the freezer for five minutes. Combine all ingredients in a shaker, shake, and strain into chilled martini glass. *Ahh.*

Index

About the Author

Aliza Kelly Faragher is a New York City–based astrologer and writer. She is the resident astrologer and occult columnist at *Allure* magazine, and her work has been featured in numerous publications including *PAPER*, *Bustle*, *BuzzFeed*, *Refinery29*, *Glamour*, and *Vice*. Aliza hosts monthly workshops and reads birth charts for private clients. She can be found at AlizaKelly.com.